BORDER PATROL

Commander Alvin Edward Moore

Sunstone Press
Santa Fe, New Mexico

DEDICATION

*This book is dedicated to the memory of my dear wife,
Laura Belle Van Zandt Moore. You are a heroine of
these pages, for you always backed me strongly in my
stormy days in the early United States Border Patrol.
We lived in an Ivory Tower — you and I, and Love.*

All of the characters in this book
are fictitious, and any resemblance
to actual persons, living or dead,
is purely coincidental.

Cover art by Brian Hough

First Edition

Printed in the United States of America

Library of Congress Cataloging in Publication Data:

Moore, Alvin Edward.
    Border patrol / Commander Alvin Moore. -- 1st ed.
        p.   cm.
    ISBN 0-86534-113-3
    1. United States. Immigration Border Patrol--History--Fiction.
I. Title.
PS3563.0569B67   1987
813'.54--dc19   87-16004
                                              CIP

Published in 1988 by SUNSTONE PRESS
                Post Office Box 2321
                Santa Fe, NM 87504-2321 / USA

CONTENTS

FOREWORD

The heroic story of the dangerous infancy of the United States
Border Patrol has never been published. An especially dangerous,
often fatal, area of its early work was the Arizona-Mexico border.
And there, seeking adventure and local color due to my nature and
literary ambition, is where I served as a young, armed Patrol Inspec-
tor, nearly sixty-one years ago.

I have been twice in the Navy, went to the Naval Academy at six-
teen and later resigned. While I was out of the Navy I was in various
U.S. official capacities, including my service on the Border Patrol.

In what spare time I could snatch from my long hours of duty I
wrote down a series of short stories based on my adventurous ex-
periences of that time. I have kept them all these years, and now at
last I have incorporated them in this story of Richard Morton.

Commander Alvin Edward Moore
30 May 1986

CHAPTER 1
A Manhunt On the Border

Like many others I, too, felt the urge to go "west" and when still a young married man I decided to give up my position as a patent examiner in Washington, D.C. and become a member of the newly formed U.S. Border Patrol. I asked for assignment on the Arizona-Mexico border, an area of our country which was still primitive.

Irving F. Wixon, Superintendent of the Border Patrol, listened to my request and then warned me. "They're having a tough time down there on the Mexican border. One of our men was killed there only last week. Our men had a fight with some smugglers. The smugglers got away but then ambushed our men when they were on the way back and Inspector McKee was killed. Do you want this job?" He looked sternly at me.

I did not hesitate. "I certainly do, sir. That is just the kind of adventurous life I am looking for. And I speak Spanish."

So it was that my wife, Laura, and I left the east and drove across country in a second-hand Chevrolet; taking the southern route, over primitive roads and sometimes using crude ferries to cross the rivers.

At length we arrived at the Border Patrol station in Nogales, Arizona. Here only a wire fence separated the United States and Mexico. At the two main streets there were gaps, called *Garitas* or Gates for legally-crossing Americans and Mexicans. Away from these *Garitas* there were occasional holes at the base of the fence, made by illegally-entering aliens. And a mile or so on each side of the Gates the fence ended; and then for many miles the barren, strangely attractive semi-desert extended. Cactus-studded, uninhabited, in seeming invitation to a dangerous course by alien or U.S. smugglers and the poor, *pelado* Mexican who desperately wanted to enter *los estados Unidos del Norte,* but didn't have enough money to pay his "headtax" and guarantee that he would not become a "public

5

charge."

We arrived late in the afternoon, and stayed our first night there in a tourist camp on the northern outskirts of the town. That night we heard the weird calls of the coyotes out in the desert. Their eerie barks and howls, sending electric vibrations through the starry night, frightened Laura, and strangely, atavistically, appealed to me. For I was seeking the wild, and I had found it.

After a week in Nogales, I was assigned to duty at a little Border Patrol station in the cattle-ranch and mining village of Patagonia, twenty-two miles north of the Border. I was fascinated by the primitive little town, and the barren, mostly uninhabited country around it. On the thousands-of-acre ranches real, not movie, cowboys rode for miles on end without seeing other human beings. Frequently bowlegged, they were dressed in faded denim, leather jackets, cactus-lacerated chaps and scuffed high-heeled boots.

The high hills around were just as barren as when they were created, and the cactus-filled desert just as cruel. In winter the sun beat down, pleasantly warm, nearly every day; and in the summer came the short rainy season. Then there was a quiet brief spring of green hills and valleys, and an amazing, short-lived splendor of flaming cactus and other desert flowers.

There were only thirty-nine of us patrolling and scouting the wide border strip of southern Arizona adjacent to Mexico. About half were ex-cowmen; and most of the remainder were veterans of the Army and Marine Corps in World War I. A veteran of the Marine Corps, a tall, slim Southerner named Martin, had a gunfight sometime after my arrival, emerged unwounded but killed his adversary. The other representative of the Navy beside myself, "Shorty" Darling, just before my arrival was chasing a carload of aliens on a motorcycle when he was forced off an embankment, had a broken neck, and was partially disabled for life.

Only four Patrol Inspectors were assigned to our Patagonia station. I met two of them my first afternoon there: our leader, Jewell Trask; and a former Army Sergeant named Gus Steinborn. Jewell Trask was the Old West incarnate. He reminded me of a hero in a Zane Grey novel. Small and wiry, he had an earnest, frank-eyed look that seemed to indicate he had never been afraid of anything. He and a man similar in appearance, but with a non-serious, humorous outlook, Lou Stevens, the Mounted Customs Inspector at Patagonia who often worked with us, had one thing quite in common: both swore by the already somewhat old-fashioned Frontier Colt forty-five revolver. I asked Lou once why he used this simple old firearm instead of the automatic, and his reply was, "When I pull a trigger I want something to go *off!*"

Jewell was an ex-cowboy of the old school, probably the best officer and pistol marksman I have ever known. I have seen him in succession knock over a row of six empty forty-five shells at thirty paces as fast as he could fire from the hip. His hands moved like lightning in "fanning" the hammer of his old single-action gun.

Gus Steinborn also was a prototype of the old, in his case, a tough sergeant of the Army Cavalry of the Old West. A medium-sized, rather stocky man, he talked bluntly, earnestly; and greatly valued his over twenty years in the Army. He seemed hard as nails but I rather liked old Gus. I learned he was married to a Mexican woman, and had a house full of *chimacos,* Mexican-American children who looked more Mexican than North American.

Lawrence Sipe, the other officer at the station, was a tall, lanky, easy-going World War I veteran, a native of Arizona. After serving with him a while I believed he would have talked slowly if arguing with the Devil against going to Hell.

When I reported for duty in Arizona there was no Border Patrol badge there for me. But soon I got one, the badge that had been worn by one of our Patrol Inspectors, another native Arizonan by the name of Lon Parker. Lon was one of the few Inspectors who patrolled the border on horseback.

We were advised only to scout in pairs but most of us from time to time *would* work alone. Lon, a well-liked youngish man, scouting alone on a trail some thirty miles north of the border, was ambushed by an alien smuggler, and killed.

We could piece out some of what happened by the mute evidence left behind by the dead officer. There were two of the Mexican smugglers. One was riding ahead, leading a pack horse, while the other hid behind a big boulder. When Lon rode by after the one ahead, the hidden smuggler opened fire, fatally shot Lon in the back, and escaped. Lon shot and killed the man ahead and his pack horse. Then he managed to ride on up the trail to a prospector's cabin. But the prospector was not at home and Lon fell from his horse, and died there.

It was a Sunday, but I was on duty at the station. Smugglers, and in those days border patrolmen, had no off-duty Sundays. It was one of those rare, rainy days of summer, when the desert turns to mud. On such a day one realizes that the customary warmth of the Southwest comes from the seldom-failing sun. Blot it out by a few days of rain, and the mountains become a miserable place of cold.

I had been checking traffic down the road; and on my return to the little one-room adobe hut of the station, I was summoned to the hotel, where the only telephone in town could be found.

I strode into the hotel out of the rain, green-uniformed, pistol belted to my side. The manner in which I wore the heavy .45 would have told I was no far-west westerner before ever I opened my mouth, for my patrol-issued belt was buckled tightly about my waist, holding my top-closed official holster and revolver high, with the handle well above the waistline. The dyed-in-the-wool westerner buckles his belt loosely and his gun sags low at his right hip in an open-top holster and in easy reach of his quick hand. It didn't take me long to adopt that fashion, for there was survival in it.

"Mrs. Farley, I came to answer the phone," I said to the proprietress.

She stared at me. "I *sent* for Lawrence Sipe," she said in a slightly acrid tone.

Mrs. Farley's reply nettled me a little. Being recently from the east, I was very sensitive to the western clannishness that an easterner met at every turn, until he had lived long enough in that frontier country to absorb some of its ways. I was on duty at the time, not Sipe, and the call had to do with the business of the Border Patrol.

"Sipe is asleep, off watch, and Jewell Trask is on a trip. But I'll answer the phone."

"Well," she said, as if washing her hands of the matter. "There it is."

I walked to the shelf that served as the hotel desk, turned the bell handle and picked up the receiver.

A far-away voice responded to my hello. "Who is this speaking?"

"This is Morton at Patagonia," I said.

"Morton? Who's Morton?"

"Morton of the Border Patrol."

"But I *asked* for Lawrence Sipe!" said the voice, sharply.

"Sipe has turned in, worn out, and I was on watch, so I came. Can't I take the message?"

Then I heard the voice relaying what I had said to someone else.

I thought, whoever is responsible for the call apparently does not know how to use a telephone. A cowpuncher, maybe.

"Hello," said the voice. "Albert Gatlin says rout Lawrence out even if he *is* asleep. And tell him to go to Canilla Pass and Parker Canyon and patrol the line east to Campaña Mesa. They got a tip that the Mexican that killed Lon Parker is gonna try to make it to Mexico tonight. And tell Lawrence to take along Jim Kane, and anybody else he can get."

"I, for one, will be going with him," I said, with irritation at being left out of the naming. "Who is this speaking anyway? Why doesn't Gatlin talk for himself?"

"This is the ranger station on top of Santa Rita Peak. The wires are down out of Loquiel, and I'm relaying the message."

There was further conversation between the ranger station and Loquiel, and then once more came the voice of the ranger. "Albert says be awful careful who you shoot. There'll be a posse out of Nogales patrolling on foot to Campaña Mesa, and you might meet 'em. Now do you get it all?"

At mention of the word "shoot," I had a thrill, or was it a *chill,* of anticipation. At that time I had fired a revolver very little. But as a member of the Naval Academy Rifle Squad I had learned to handle a rifle rather well and in fact had qualified as a Navy "Expert Marksman." But I questioned my ability to hit a man in the dark. Most of my Navy training had been for group fighting, shoulder to shoulder with comrades, not alone on a trackless desert, with only coyotes for witnesses. On the other hand, the Mexican killer would cheerfully murder his assailant in cold blood, step across the line and report it among his *compadres* as a great exploit — putting another *gringo* out of the way. But, notwithstanding my doubts of competence in this violent game of survival or death, I replied with a firm voice, as no doubt, have millions of soldiers on the eve of their first battle. As my grandfather doubtless did before the terrible Civil War battle of Shiloh.

"Let's see now," I said. "We're to go to Canilla Pass, start at Parker Canyon and patrol east to Campañna Mesa. That right?"

"Yep. And stay out till after sunup, Albert says. He may come through late. Well, I reck'n that's all. Goodbye."

Back at the little adobe station, I was met by Hugh Walker, Immigration Inspector at Nogales, who with his wife was visiting Laura and me. Hugh was a nervy, wiry little fellow, the type of adventurer who jumped into the war on the side of the Allies before the United States entered. An ex-airman, he reminded me of nothing so much as a restless bird. I believe that a person's pets usually reflect his own personality; Hugh's were a couple of bellicose little bantum roosters that licked the whole feathered neighborhood.

"Well, what's up?" he demanded.

"Got to patrol the line for that murderer!"

"Golly, I wish I could go with you!" Hugh ejaculated.

"No, you do *not!*" interposed his wife. "I'm not wanting any husband of mine shot by a Mexican."

"Nor I," said my wife. "I don't see why you have to go away off on this rainy night anyway."

"I'm paid for it," I said. "And I have to get a move on. See you all again."

When I knocked, Lawrence Sipe came to the door of his adobe house dressed in pajamas. For a day and a half he had not slept. All day and night before he had ridden over the rain-soaked mountains, searching in vain for the murderer.

Although he had just returned an hour or so before, with a tired body crying for sleep, he made no complaint when I gave him Gatlin's message. I soon learned that to go two, three or even four nights without much sleep was a common experience in the Border Patrol.

"Get dressed," I said, "and I'll wake Jim Kane, get my car and come back for you."

Jim Kane was the perennial Deputy Sheriff at Patagonia. A short, stocky man with the blue eyes and blond hair typical of many Irish, and yet with something of the Latin in his countenance. His grandfather, one of the earliest American pioneers in Arizona, had married a Mexican woman.

Jim seemed not too eager to make the trip and asked who had ordered him to go along. I told him Albert Gatlin had sent for him. He grumbled some more, and finally emerged on his porch. He was dressed in typical cowboy costume, bibless overalls, leather jerkin and high-heeled cowboy boots that clanked at his every step. He carried a sheathed carbine and an overcoat.

Without much conversation we got in my car, picked up Sipe, who was waiting by the road with his Winchester, and soon left the little town's cluster of adobe houses.

I turned down a little used road to the southeast, with the

headlights carving a long slice of mud from out of the surrounding darkness. It had rained all day, and now the air was heavy with the chill dampness of a rainy season night. Before long it would be freezing cold.

Poor Sipe, who had taken the back seat, soon was fast asleep, snoring noisily.

The road became worse and worse, requiring the entire attention of Jim Kane and myself. Jim picked the way, giving from memory warning information of ravines and washed-out places ahead, while I tried to keep the car going forward over the slick mud.

At length, coming to a stretch of comparatively level ground, we fell to discussing the death of Lon Parker.

"A fine boy was Lon," said Jim. "Sure was a good boy, and a good officer. I sure hated to hear about him dying. Me and him was raised together on the same ranch, and ate out of the same beanpot. Yes, I knew him well. He wasn't afraid of the Devil himself."

"He was too rash they say," I said. "Always going out by himself after a whole gang of smugglers. Sipe tells me that last fall he rode fast ahead of two other officers in a chase for some Mexican smugglers, got into a shooting scrape, and killed one and captured the others before the other two men could come up. Now, you know a man like that is bound to get it sooner or later. He might just as well have waited for those other two men."

"Yes, and he might have lost the smugglers. Who knows? No, a man in this work has to go it alone a lot, and just take his chances. Every man on the Border Patrol gets into a shooting scrape sooner or later. The worst part about poor old Lon is it took a shot in the back to get him. Sipe said he crawled about a hundred yards on his hands and knees before he got to that prospector's cabin. And then the old man wasn't home. Wasn't that tough! So he dies out by the wood pile; and his horse and his old dog stuck to him through it all."

"Did Sipe say his gun was loaded?"

"Yes, he said it was fully loaded. Lon must have reloaded it after he shot that Mexican, and he must have shot the fellow after he was already mortally wounded, himself. What a lot of grit he had! He died like a *man!*"

"I guess the Mexican and the horse he shot were used as a bait to draw him into the ambush, so the other Mexican could kill him."

"I suppose so. No one'll ever know, for sure. If Lon hadn't shot the Mexican we wouldn't know anything. They found tracks where the other man had stood, and then run away. It's a dead certainty that this man Sanchez did the killing. Like a fool, he went up to Fort Huachuca and bragged to two *amigos* about it. One didn't happen to be so good an *amigo* as he thought. This one told the Sheriff, and the Sheriff went to Sanchez' house. Sanchez was in back. As soon as he saw the Sheriff, he tore out through the mesquite and got away."

The front wheels suddenly pitched downward and the springs slapped together.

"What the hell!" came from the back seat, and Sipe sat up, his eyes full of sleep. "Where are we?"

"Just crossed Harshaw Canyon," said Kane. "San Rafael Valley is just ahead." He added for my benefit, "Over the mountain."

We now began to wheel-crawl up the face of what appeared to be a cliff. The air grew cold and thin and it seemed to me as if the top of the world had been reached. Then at last we crossed through Canilla Pass and passed beyond into San Rafael Valley.

Actually, there was little valley to it, beyond a shallow level basin, over a mile high, with mountains for a rim. The crescent moon had just risen, and by its ghostly light I could discern the plateau stretching away to the right, as far as the eye could see — empty, desolate, into dim nothingness. Like an inland sea it looked to me, lonely and level under the moonlight, with a monotony that was broken only by the mast of a far distant, "ship," a tall cottonwood tree, and a "wave" far away that was a slight rise of barren ground.

"Down there's the line," said Jim Kane, pointing to the right.

I looked once toward Mexico, and then bent all my energies on driving. Down the incline we plunged, the wheels skidding dangerously half the time.

But at last we came to level ground once more. *Too* level, it proved to be, for the water running down the mountains for two days had sunk deep into the pasty soil, making one great muddy morass of the trail. It was hub deep in places, but we kept forging steadily ahead for some two or three miles.

Then we came to a bad place where the wheels sank deeper than ever and rebelled against further movement. Sipe and Kane jumped out to push, while I stepped on the accelerator to the floorboard.

Poor Sipe sleepily made the mistake of getting behind one of the rear wheels, and his face was plastered with black mud. He cursed and pushed all the harder, but to no avail. The car would not move.

Lights from two other machines appeared a mile or so behind us.

By the time they came up, Sipe was thoroughly awake, and both he and Kane were sweating but the car had not advanced an inch. The two arriving cars carried Albert Gatlin's group, augmented by a posse of officers from Douglas County. By their aid, we soon got my car out of the mud and to a safe place beyond. Shutting off the motor, I got out and joined the others. In the dim light the little knot of men looked rough and ready with their boldly carved faces, almost universally in need of a shave, and their worn khaki trousers over high-heeled boots.

They talked among themselves, about Lon Parker's lonely death, about this rancher and that miner, while I stood at the edge of the group, not spoken to and not speaking, as if isolated on a desert island. They were interested only in each other, in their west, their Arizona — not in an easterner with eastern ways and eastern manners of speech. I had not been long enough in their country, had not proved my merit in western things according to the unwritten code of these old-style westerners.

"Well, it's getting late," Albert said. "Reckon we'd better get started. How much gas you got in that car, Jim?"

"It's not mine, it's Mr. Morton's here," Kane replied.

"Filled it up this afternoon," I said.

"Reckon you'll have to go the farthest then," said Albert Gatlin. "These other two cars haven't got much gas. Well, I'll get in this car here and take the men out, as I reckon I know the country better than anybody else. You other two cars follow, and when all the men in this car are gone, I'll get out and get in the one behind. You come last, Mr. Morton."

"By the way," he continued. "There's an extra rifle in here — anybody need one?"

I was the only man there who did not have his own pet rifle.

"Yeah," said Sipe. "Mr. Morton here ain't got a rifle."

Albert brought it to me, a Winchester, in an untanned leather scabbard.

"All right, boys, let's go!" he said easily, and crawled into the forward car. "All I've got to say, men, is if you see anybody comin' toward the line tonight, yell at 'em in English. And if he don't answer in English, shoot! It's either that or get shot with this fellow. Damn him, if I wasn't an officer, I'd shoot him like a rattler. He didn't yell did he, before he shot poor old Lon through the back. The son-of-a-bitch!" His voice became husky.

13

I learned later that Lon and Albert had fought together in several gunfights on the Border. Lon had been as near to Gatlin as his own brother, and his murder had all but turned him from an impartial officer into an avenging Nemesis.

"If he don't answer in English, shoot!" The phrase ran through my mind long after the little caravan was proceeding down the valley.

We came to a dim trail extending at right angles to our course, and the leading car turned to the left.

"This road runs along the line," said Jim Kane.

Presently, the forward car stopped. A man got out and stalked away toward the line, tall, slim and straight, with a rifle held in his right hand. He must have been a rancher, deputized for the occasion, for he was clothed in overalls and jumper.

Ranchers, turning out of bed to patrol the line at night! I was reminded of stories of the old-time border. Surely, it had changed but little down here at its middle. A grim business this, with the determined figures of ranchers and officers stalking off in the moonlight, rifles ready, prepared to shoot and be shot at. The east seemed far away, indeed.

The cavalcade started again only to stop a half mile or so farther to let out another figure to walk off into the night. And so on, until all the men in the forward car but Albert Gatlin were posted. Then Gatlin came back to the second car and the process was repeated; men dropping off at canyon, ridge and mesa, and the last one, the driver, staying by his car.

So, at last, Albert joined our group. I foresaw with some uneasiness that, being the driver of the last car, I would be the ultimate man of this long patrol, the last trap of this human trapline. I did not like the idea; it would have pleased me more to have a neighbor on each side.

Some distance farther, a ranch house came into view, the first we had seen on this trail that parallelled the line. No lights were visible, and all was quiet. Apparently the family was in bed.

"Stop here and we'll get another man," said Albert.

As I halted the car in front of the house, hoarse-throated dogs shattered the stillness of the night.

Albert got out and went in. The dogs recognized him and hushed immediately. I thought, probably every dog for fifty miles along the border knows Albert Gatlin.

One long, lean hound had come out through a hole in the fence and now growled at the car in menacing fashion, as if uncertain whether or not these were Albert's friends.

"*Cállate!*" snapped Sipe, and the dog slunk away. "Must've been a Mexican dog sometime," he said.

There was a stir within and presently Albert returned, accompanied by a sturdy rancher in overalls, jumper and high-heeled boots, carrying the usual Winchester.

"Alright," Albert said, with no introduction of the newcomer to me. We drove on.

A quarter of a mile went by, and the man dropped off, having said no more than half a dozen words; all I learned about him was his first name was Bill.

A few minutes later Jim Kane also left us, and farther on, a half mile or so, Lawrence Sipe got off in a canyon. This left only Albert Gatlin and myself. It seemed to me that we were going to the end of space — or the end of the United States, which seemed the same thing to me at the time.

"What's the name of this place?" I asked to make conversation.

"This is *La Boca* canyon. That means "The Mouth," you know; it's where most of the smugglers come through. I doubt though if our man will come through here; it's too much used. A little ahead is Campaña Mesa — a likely spot. You can stop there with your car, if you want to. I'll go on about a half-mile to the next big canyon. The trail gets worse from here on, so I'll walk."

I did not reply, for suddenly I was concentrating all my attention on trying to avoid a wreck. We had suddenly plunged down a short and exceedingly steep hill, as slippery as glass. It was very rocky also, and was bounded by a sheer precipice close to the left. In trying to lessen the terrific momentum acquired on the slope, I applied the brakes. The hind wheels locked in a skid and the rear of the car swung to the left toward the brink. I rapidly chose the lesser of two evils and acted in a flash of subconscious thought. Releasing the brakes, I stepped hard on the accelerator and the car sprang to the right with a roar. Off the road we plunged, and down the hill like a shot, bouncing from rocks and holes until it seemed that the springs must break. At last we reached the bottom of the ravine and the front of the car bounded several feet in the air as we started up the other side.

I swung back into the road and stepped on the power to climb the hill. But it was too slippery. The wheels began to spin. Shifting into second, I had a little better luck, slowly climbing upward.

"You qualify for desert driving," said Albert, quietly; and I warmed with pleasure at this first bit of praise from a western man.

We were now on Campaña Mesa, a wide, flat tableland, barren of everything save sparse grass. And a short distance farther, Albert asked me to stop the car.

"No need of going off the trail," he said. "You can just sit in your car and keep watch right here. The line runs parallel to this road, off there to the right. If you look close, you can see a white border monument way off there to the left. See? He'll have to cross this trail somewhere, if he comes through. He could cross here."

He got out and started to go. I was sorry to see him leave.

"I may walk down aways," I said. "So be sure it's not me before you shoot down the trail."

"Oh no; I won't shoot down the trail. He'll never stay on this trail He'll just cross it, that's all. Well, I've got to get going. I'll be back about sunup."

I stared after his broad retreating form, until it dissolved into the moonlight. A queer feeling of uneasiness that was akin to fright, and yet not fright, possessed me. It was not that I feared being shot by a renegade Mexican, for in a sense, I did not. It was the solitude of it all. The utter desolation of the weirdly beautiful night scene combined with the ghosts of all the stories I had read of lone fights fought out between man and man, with only the western stars for witnesses, and coyotes for grave-diggers, had a strange effect on me.

For hours I sat in nervous tension on the front seat of my car and stared to the northward, my eyes sweeping around in a semicircular arc, with the trail for its chord. Across this trail somewhere the murderer would come; and I intended not to let him cross it here unseen.

Over and over, I planned what I would do. Fortunately the rain had stopped. I would get out of the car, and advance to meet the oncoming man. And when near enough, I would yell, "Halt!" Then if the other shot, I would shoot.

But what if the murderer did not open fire, but ran instead? It would clearly be my duty to get him dead or alive, but would I? I tortured myself with such questions. What if the alien saw me before I could get out of the car, and opened fire on the front seat? He would have an easy mark. Furthermore, what if Mexican smugglers cross the line into the United States from behind me? Would I be able to cope with them alone? Thinking of this contingency, I began to look toward Mexico, also, and now my gaze comprised an entire circle of dim horizon.

As far as I could see, there was nothing but a flat stretch of tableland, unpeopled, devoid of trees. By the moonlight, the mesa seemed like a limitless desert.

My gaze constantly shifted from north to south and from south to north. Never had I stood lookout watch at sea more assiduously. Finally, on one of my periodic northward swings, I detected something that sent a cold chill up and down my spine. What was that, far off there to the north? Or was my imagination playing tricks?

I stared and stared. And then I saw it again. It moved, an unmistakable *something*. Or was it a mere shadow? No, it moved again, and then it seemed to melt away into nothingness. For over half an hour I crouched there, rifle in hand, staring, straining my eyes trying to see something I was not sure I had seen.

Midnight came and went; and the mountain air, chilled by the heavy rains, grew biting-cold. My teeth began to chatter. My body was cramped; my feet went to sleep.

For hours, it seemed, I sat there, almost motionless. I tried to relax my tensed muscles. And then again I saw a shadow in the distance. My heart leaped, for now it was nearer. And it looked as though it might be a horse. And a rider? But then the long drawn-out bellow of a bull shattered the stillness. And I sat back. Open-range cattle were out there feeding, making the situation all the more complex. How was I to tell whether a shape was a cow or a murderer's horse? I decided there was no way. I either had to take my chances, or else transform the night into a Fourth-of-July with my fireworks. All I could do, it seemed, was to sit there, and freeze and watch, alert for anything. There was no danger whatever of my going to sleep. In fact, I had never felt less sleepy in my life than on that particular early morning.

And so, there I sat, freezing and hardly knowing I froze, while the seconds, and minutes, and hours dragged past. It seemed to me that I counted each a dozen times.

At last, about four o'clock, it became so cold that I got out of the car to walk, Winchester in hand. And then it happened! A rifle cracked, and a bullet smashed through the window of my car.

I strained my eyes to keenly search the moonlit spaces to the north. And in the distance I saw him on foot. "Maybe a hundred yards," I muttered. And I dropped to my doubled-up right knee on the wet ground, rested my left elbow and hand holding the Winchester on my bent left knee, in one of the accurate rifle-shooting positions I long ago learned. Calm now, I very carefully aimed that old Winchester and squeezed the trigger. I fired and I was *pleased* to see the man fall.

I grabbed a cord that, in lieu of handcuffs, I had brought on the front seat of the car. And cautiously I moved toward the prostrate figure. As I came close to him I kept my revolver trained on him — taking no chances of his jumping up and attacking with a knife.

But he was obviously deathly wounded. And he had his hands raised in mute surrender. "*Socorro, Señor*" he pleaded. "Help!"

Silently I drew his hands together, and with the cord tightly tied his wrists together. Then I said in Spanish: "Is your name Sanchez?"

"*Si, Señor.*"

"Then you're under arrest for the murder of Lon Parker."

"But if I die, Señor — *qué le hace!*"

I saw that he was shot through the chest — but not through the heart — and was bleeding rather profusely. I took out my handkerchief and tried to staunch the flow. But the cloth became very wet with blood. So I took my pocketknife and cut a handful of the sparse grass; and this I stuffed deep into the bullet-hole. It seemed to help. I realized the blood was from a vein, not an artery.

Then I got my car, drove to the man, and managed to get him on the back seat. He lay there on his side, like a hurt animal, silently enduring.

I blew my horn three times in succession. But I knew that if Albert Gatlin hadn't heard the rifle shots he wouldn't hear the horn. Anyway, daybreak must be near; and I settled back to wait. But the cold was so intense that I got out of the car to walk.

Early dawn brought Albert, carbine in hand, stalking over the mesa. We met. "I heard shooting," he said. "Did you shoot?"

"Yes. And Albert, I have that murderer on the back seat!"

Surprised, he went to the car, and looked at the wounded man. His flow of blood seemed to be stopping — a mere slight ooze now.

"You qualify for the Patrol," Albert said. "He'll live. But it's too bad you didn't kill the son-of-a-bitch. It would have saved the Government a lot of trouble and money. To hang him or else board him for life."

I didn't answer. But I thought, I'm glad I missed his heart. He probably has to be executed — but if he is, I don't want to be his executioner.

The murderer lived. But he was sentenced to be "hanged by the neck until dead."

And that is the story of my first manhunt and my first gunfight in the dangerous infancy of the United States Border Patrol.

CHAPTER 2
Dark Jim

Soon after I arrived at my first Border Patrol station in the mining and ranch village of Patagonia, I thoroughly realized that the new State of Arizona was still the Old West of cowmen, prospectors, miners, six-guns and Winchesters, and above all its wilderness. Man was only an alien here, a mere late camper on the fringes of the Great Loneliness out there. That lone area appealed to the basic solitariness of my nature: by night a million sparkling jewels in the sky and a moon that nearly always could be seen; by day bright sunshine, clear bracing air, and lonely purple peaks across the semi-desert in the distance. It seldom rained here; and when it did men and animals were thankful, and the desert suddenly and briefly blazed with colorful beauty. I loved it all; and I knew I had come to the right place.

One day my new friend, Earl Thompson, principal of the small high school at Patagonia, said: "Morton, you want local color. I know a man who can supply you with plenty of it. His name is James Statton, and his nickname will tell you what an interesting character he is: 'Dark Jim', an old prospector, strictly of the Old West. He's just come to town again for supplies. Alone, out there, he's read a lot; and surprisingly he speaks pretty good English. He'll talk a lot if he knows you well enough. Want to meet him?"

"I certainly do. I've seen him and his burro at the General Store."

A short time later we found him.

"Dark Jim," Earl said, "I want you to meet a friend of mine, Border Patrol Inspector, Richard Morton. Mr. Morton, this is Mr. Statton."

"Howdy," the old man said, extending a gnarled hand.

I could see that here was authentic stuff, one of the lone breed of wandering prospectors who had helped open the Old West to such imperfect civilization as we have struggled to attain. What a character! A seamed dark face with a slow, forthright look apparently marked by the Great Lonesome of the barren spaces. Tall, wiry and old, in faded blue jumper and faded blue trousers, the ends of which were stuffed in scarred, heavy boots. Wearing an old narrow-brimmed felt hat, with the front edge pulled down. Beneath that brim was the most peculiar part of his appearance: his face. One not easily to be forgotten; of dusky, almost black, hue. His nose was aquiline, and finely chiseled except for a nick, apparently a knife scar, which marred the right nostril. His gray eyes were deep-set, squinted by years in the bright western sun; and his lips were rather thin, stern-looking. I learned later that he was of old-time American parentage. Those features ordinarily would inspire trust and confidence; but there was that dark screen between them and the observer that negated any good impression. The darkness of his skin, ominous as a black cloud on an otherwise good day. Dark Jim! Probably a throwback to some swarthy member of an ancient, invading horde from Asia.

"There are tales about Dark Jim," Earl had said. "Probably mostly about his youth which apparently was sometimes violent. This country has *not* been easy to tame, you know. And I'd say Dark Jim has a dangerous-looking face."

And so he had. Maybe I can get a good story from him, I thought.

In the next few days before Dark Jim resumed his solitary wandering, I saw as much of him as my Border Patrol duties would permit. He seemed to like me, and twice came and sat on the porch, feet on the ground, of our little adobe station while I checked traffic coming up from the Mexican border, looking for illegal aliens or smugglers. We talked some about books but I sought to steer our conversation to the subject of his past. And so I managed to get an interesting story from him. My hope is that in passing it on I can aid some in preserving the memory of that vanishing breed of lone, sturdy, individualistic prospectors. This was his story.

While mixing sourdough batter, Dark Jim suddenly raised his head and listened intently. Approaching footsteps! Some cowpuncher, perhaps, looking for wild cattle? Presently around a bend in the wide canyon came a burro, a patient, stoical little burro, much like Dark Jim's own, and loaded with an outfit similar to Dark Jim's: bedding, cooking utensils, provisions, covered with a tarpaulin; and not the customary single rifle but two. Behind the burro walked a strange person.

He was tall and lanky, dressed in a sheepskin coat, khaki breeches, boots and a mishapen, black felt hat. His dark-white face was long, cavernous, his nose long and his lips thin, the upper lip concealed by a long, ferocious-looking mustache, slick and dark as night. His hair, too, was of this blackish shade, slick and long, hanging below the collar of his sheepskin coat. As he approached closer, Dark Jim could see beneath his coat the gun handles of two six-shooters.

"Howdy, partner," said the newcomer. "Water handy here?"

"Sure," said Dark Jim. "Camp."

The stranger drove his burro off the trail and began to unpack.

"Reckon you're prospecting, ain't you?" inquired the long-haired man, after they had eaten supper and washed the dishes, Dark Jim doing most of the work and the stranger most of the eating. Jim puffed at his pipe, removed it from his mouth, and looked at the other, sitting crosslegged, framed in the black background of the night beyond.

"Yeah, a little. Thought I'd take a little trip."

"You're an old hand at that game, I reckon."

"Well, I've done a little of it, off and on," Dark Jim modestly said. "What's your line of work; you ain't a prospector, are you?"

"Oh, I do a little of everything," said the stranger. "Just now I'm looking for something to do."

"Funny place you come to look for a job."

"Yeah, so it is. But a good place, I reckon, if you don't want to have no doings with the damn settlements and their damn law. Say, what do you expect to find out in these mountains in the way of mines anyhow?"

"Silver or lead mostly here in this country. By a lucky chance, *maybe* gold."

"Gold!"

"Yeah, gold."

"Reckon I'd like to find a gold mine, myself. What's the chances of me going along with you? I know how to pan and I'll do my part of the work; and I got about the same size outfit as you got."

"Sure. Glad to have you along."

"What's your name?" the stranger asked.

"Jim Statton; but everybody calls me Dark Jim."

"Well, my name's Stern — Aleck Stern — anyhow that's what I go by. I'm in this country for my health," he added significantly tapping the butt of one of his heavy revolvers. "Shake hands, *partner.*"

"Listen," said Dark Jim a while later. "Ain't that a horse coming?"

"Sounds like it, don't it?" said the longhaired Aleck Stern, in a strained voice, laying his hands on his pistols, which were still belted to his side.

They waited, Aleck Stern's long face grimly set, and presently a horse and rider emerged from the darkness into the circle of firelight. He rode up and dismounted with a jingle of spurs. He was dressed in typical rancher's clothing: a wide hat with brim turned up along the right edge, forming a sharp apex in front, blue jumper, cactus-scarred "chaps," and high-heeled cowboy boots. Beneath the hat, in a square, red face, pale blue eyes looked out on the world with the frank, trustful curiosity of a child. He took hold of the forward curled-up portion of the brim of his hat and, with what seemed an habitual gesture, lifted it, scratched his head with his thumb, and carefully replaced the hat. Drawling at the same time in a low, intimate tone, "Howdy, boys."

"Howdy," responded Dark Jim.

Aleck Stern, who looked at the newcomer with a hard, relentless stare, did not reply.

The cowman let his eyes slowly take in the camp, the two burros and the two pack outfits.

"Sit down and make yourself at home," said Dark Jim. "Had supper?"

"Yeah, had supper, thank you," said the stranger, sitting down crosslegged. "I was just going on home, when I saw your fire and thought I'd stop by. So doggone few people come through here, you know. Reckon you all are prospecting, eh?"

"Yeah, thought maybe we might find something up in the Glories," said Dark Jim. "I didn't know there was anybody living round here. Where's your ranch?"

"About five miles down toward the way you come. Been there four years now, and I'm gonna leave pretty soon. 'Bout starved out."

"Looks like you got a little more stuff than them burros can pack," observed the rancher a little later. "Don't you want another burro?"

"Well, my burro is overloaded," admitted Dark Jim. "Especially for the ground we're going over. But I guess we can get by."

"I don't mean I want to sell a burro. I've got one down in my pasture 'bout half wild that you can have for nothin' if you can ketch him. If you can ever git a pack on him, he'll be all right, I reckon. I ain't got no use for him at all."

"What do you think about staying over and getting him?" Dark Jim asked Aleck Stern.

"I think five miles is too far to go back," said Aleck, sulkily.

"Well, it ain't five miles," said the rancher. "It's only about four miles to the pasture. You know that big canyon you crossed when you first hit the valley? Turn down it and it's about a mile down."

"I think we'd better stay and get that burro, Stern," said Dark Jim. "We need him, don't you think?" And in the end they decided to do so, Aleck Stern for some reason seeming not to relish the thought of turning back at all.

On the following day they got up before daylight, broke camp, packed the burros and set out to retrace their steps. Following the hospitable rancher's directions, they went down the canyon and found the pasture, which was fenced in by two strands of barbed wire, nailed to growing mesquite trees and in places where there were no trees, to gnarled mesquite posts. At length they found the burro and he was as wild as the wildest of his progenitors. The minute he saw them he smelled the pack saddle, and undesirous of the lowly servitude of the ass, broke into a wild run. Despite all their efforts, he broke through their cordon, not far from Aleck Stern, and ran with a speed that would have made a veteran mule driver wonder at the little animal, to the farthest corner of the field, where he stopped and nonchalantly proceeded to graze on the sparse grass.

Dark Jim followed with the stoical patience so characteristic of him, while behind, unwillingly and slowly, came his new partner, cursing the donkey family, from the Mexican burro to the Missouri jackass, and threatening to kill this particular member of it. He suggested to Dark Jim that they do without the burro; to which Dark Jim shook his head. "No, we ought to get him. We need him."

On the other side of the pasture they repeated the performance, the little burro again escaping. For nearly an hour they crossed and recrossed that field, Dark Jim with stoical patience, and Aleck Stern with growing profane irritation.

At length, however, they succeeded in trapping the wily, little animal in an acute-angled corner of the fence. They closed in gradually. Dark Jim advanced with rope in hand, calmly confident.

But the burro, sensing disaster, rushed toward Aleck Stern, who made a curious gesture with his hands. Then Dark Jim sprang and was in the animal's path. But the harassed burro did the unexpected. He dropped down on all fours, wriggled under the bottom strand of wire and in a moment was gone like a shot, to join his wild brothers of the hill.

Aleck Stern swore, whipped out one of his revolvers and began firing at the fleeing animal. He emptied the gun, and the burro, now trotting steadily, went down a canyon and out of sight. Aleck loaded and sheathed his pistol, and swore a long succession of foul oaths, no two alike and each worse than the last. His long black mustache bristled and his narrow, deep-set gray eyes snapped with ugly fire. Dark Jim looked at him comtemplatively. Here, evidently, was a man as fierce as he looked, who made not the slightest effort to control his sudden brutal passions and who might murder on the slightest provocation. Probably he was a fugitive from the law because of some killing committed in just such a sudden fit of anger. Dark Jim began to regret that he had agreed to the partnership. A very unpleasant companion this man probably would be during months of mountainous solitude, not only unpleasant, but as uncontrolled and dangerous as a bull ape in his moments of bestial rage. But Dark Jim was not a man to break a compact, so he turned on his heel and silently started toward the waiting pack animals.

On the afternoon of the third day, high up in the Glories, a heavy snowstorm came. They were traveling up a rocky canyon with steep walls extending up fifteen feet on both sides, and the snow hurled into their faces in cold, slanting, blinding flurries. The air was full of the fine white flakes, vision extremely imperfect, and the rocky way becoming more and more uncertain. Burros and men stumbled over the boulders and Aleck Stern cursed alternately and then jointly the weather and the rocky way.

"I'll be a son-of-a-bitch if this ain't hell! What do you say we stop?"

"No, we gotta keep going. We can't stop in this. Liable to keep up for days."

On and on they stumbled, beating the burros with broken mesquite limbs to prevent their turning tail to the storm. Up and up, while the going became rougher and rougher and the air thinner and colder. As they went Dark Jim studied both walls of the rocky gorge as well as he could in the blinding snow. At last, Aleck Stern stopped.

"I'm not going another damned step!" he said. "You can go to hell! I'm quitting this damned partnership! *Now!*" And he drove his burro behind an outcropping rock by the side of the canyon.

"Better come on, partner, you'll freeze here," patiently insisted Dark Jim.

"You go to hell I say!" exploded the other. "I'm stayin' right here. I'm not gonna climb this mountain *no* more. I'm gonna go back down soon's this snow quits."

Dark Jim stiffened. "Better come on," he reiterated. "We'll find a lot better place than this."

"No, I won't go. You go ahead, damn you! I'm through."

"Well, all right then."

The snow by now had become several inches deep and Jim's boots sank in it as in mire. Ahead, the little burro floundered with the dogged patience of its kind, not unlike the patience acquired by its master during years of driving the little stoics before him. Every so often they would approach a seemingly insurmountable barrier, but always, somehow or other, they managed to scale it and continued on. At last, however, they found one that not only seemed insurmountable but in actuality was. A sheer wall of solid rock loomed before them, elevating, in one sudden rise, the floor of the canyon from one level to another, as a lock does the surface of water in a canal. It marked the site of a waterfall in the summer rainy season and at its base was a hole, worn out of the rock by the falling water and filled with a scattering of stones, lightly covered with soft snow.

Dark Jim kicked one of the stones and saw that it was porphyritic formation. He decided to explore the canyon just a little distance farther and if he did not find a better site, to camp at the base of this miniature cliff, whose face would, after a fashion, be a shelter against the northern storm. With fingers stiff from cold in his worn gloves, he took a rope from his pack and tied the burro to a nearby mesquite. Then he retraced his steps and a short distance back ascended by way of a rocky draw to the rim of the canyon. Here the wind and snow struck him with extra violence, and he shivered a bit beneath his old Mackinaw coat. He hurried to keep warm.

Above the cliff-like barrier he again descended into the canyon, now at a higher elevation. And there before his eyes, not twenty feet away, was what he had been seeking. The mouth of a small cave in the canyon wall yawned before him.

He hurried forward and entered. The entrance was but little higher than his head and the roof sloped downward to a point about fifteen feet back. The floor was nearly level with the base of the canyon. Small it was but a haven of refuge against the storm.

He went back for his animal companion and by beatings and coaxings managed to get the burro up into the cave.

Then he went outside and after a search returned with an armful of dead wood. He would build a fire and thaw out his hands before returning to rescue his unpleasant partner from freezing. Sorting out the small sticks and pieces of bark, he arranged them for lighting and took a loose match from a waterproof package in his pocket. As his trousers were wet, he went over to the side of the cave and picked up a stone to strike the match on. He carefully brushed the snow off the rock, and holding it with his left hand and the match in his right, was on the point of striking it when something about the rock attracted his attention. In a flash he was changed from a picture of patience to incarnation of excitement. The match dropped from his fingers. Gripping the stone with both hands, he hurried to the mouth of the cave. There the light was better; and he bent over and intently studied the rock. Ah yes, it was so! Gleaming against a dull red background of porphyry was a rough piece of yellow metal. Gold!

Once more Dark Jim experienced the supreme elation of the prospector's existence. He forgot the snow, the cold and the fact that he had intended to build a fire. He forgot everything in life except the yellow metal that gleams dully and controls so many human things in life. Excitedly, he turned his eyes upward and studied the roof. At first he was disappointed. Then in a corner toward the cliff-drop outside, he saw it — a vein of that yellow glitter. He shouted into the snowy loneliness: "I found my gold mine! Gold is where you find it. And I've found it. Gold!"

Back into the teeth of the storm he plunged and back in the direction he had come he fought his way. He had decided not to keep the discovery for himself alone, even though he alone was responsible for it and even though Aleck Stern had quit.

He found Aleck huddled around a feeble fire behind the outcropping rock. Apparently in a lethargic state from the cold, he slowly turned his head as Dark Jim approached.

"Stern, I found a cave about two miles above here. We can build a fire in it and keep warm till this storm blows over."

"Ah, go on and leave me alone, I say!" exclaimed Aleck Stern. "I'm through with you and damned prospecting. Git on! Leave me be!"

"Listen Stern, I found something in that cave. It'll mean a fortune for us both. Man, there's a big gold vein there. Gold, man — gold, and gold, and gold!"

"Gold!" A magic word! In a twinkling, Aleck had thrown off his stupor. "God! Are you sure it's gold? Man, let's go before somebody else gits there!"

That night they slept in the little cave and next day the storm subsided. Dark Jim took his prospecting hammer and went out to survey his find. The warm sun of the southwest was shining on the glittering snow and melting it away.

He scaled the precipice of the little cliff, pecking here and there with his little pick. When he descended he said to Stern: "It's as good as I thought. The vein comes out on the cliff face. We could work it ourselves; but our best bet is to get some company in here to work on a big scale. Our royalties will bring us more that way than if we worked it ourselves. What do you think?"

Aleck Stern, as usual, thought the opposite. "Of course, you'll do it your way," he said sulkily. "But I believe we oughta keep it all ourselves. If we work it ourselves then we git it all."

Dark Jim thought, very little you've shown toward work of any kind. It wouldn't be 'we' at all — it'd be me! But he only said calmly, "No, Stern, I've been in the mining game long enough to know that the company's the thing for us. I'm going to get busy now and fix it up so it'll look good when the mining men come. Then we'll go back and get 'em."

Before he started to work he asked Aleck if he would go out and kill some fresh meat.

"What do I want to kill any meat for?" asked Aleck Stern in a surly tone. "We don't need any. If you want any meat, go kill it yourself."

Dark Jim said nothing as he went to work, but he thought a great deal. Never in all his years of prospecting had he known a partner so useless, so lazy, so unwilling. He regretted in the first place that he had ever taken him as a partner and in the second place that he had not let him die in the snow the day before.

All day long he labored, chipping off stone here and there, exposing the gold to better advantage. What the publicity agent does for a show he was doing for the mine; real worth was there, but it was better to expose it in the best possible light.

When at last he descended, satisfied and somewhat proud of his work, it was near nightfall and he had to cook supper. Not a hand's turn had Aleck Stern done that livelong day. All day long he had stood and sat around, part of the time watching his partner work and part of the time in the cave. Most exasperating, Jim thought.

By daylight the next morning Dark Jim was up and away, leaving Aleck Stern still sleeping. He went up the canyon, a Winchester rifle on his shoulder, taking long, steady steps in the intermittent level stretches of sandwash and snow, breathing deeply of the fresh, cold air at dawn and expelling it in clouds of vapor. For two hours he walked and climbed, unrewarded by sight of game. At the end of that time, however, he saw two yearling cows grazing on a rocky knoll to the right of the ravine he was on. Approaching closer, he made out that they were unbranded and therefore wild cattle, mavericks. Drawing a bead on the smaller, he fired and it fell.

By means of a rope he had brought, he hung the beef up in a mesquite tree, skinned it and cut off a forequarter to take back with him. Then he placed the hide up in the tree, shifted the beef higher, marked the spot in his mind's eys, and set out for camp.

As he approached the cave he saw Aleck perched halfway up the bluff industriously pecking at its stone face with the prospecting hammer. Pleasantly surprised at this evidence of work on the part of his hitherto useless companion, he drew nearer. Then he saw what Stern was doing. Holding a tobacco pouch with one hand and using the hammer with the other he was busily engaged in knocking off the gold that Dark Jim had exposed the day before, and collecting it in the pouch. Dark Jim's anger burned hot within him, clamorous for expression. But he fought to stifle it. Rage had been the cause of much trouble in his life, and long ago he had learned to curb it; and in all but the most exasperating of circumstances he entirely subdued it. He retraced his steps some distance and, to warn his partner, released a boulder to roll noisily down a slope. With a tolerance born in and fostered by a life of communion with nature, he resolved to say nothing of what he had seen, to tolerantly regard it as unimportant evidence of the weak part of Man's inheritance. After all, Aleck, at the most, could not have more than fifty dollars worth of gold in that tobacco pouch, a trifling sum compared to the fortune awaiting them, too trifling to fight over. Time and again he had witnessed destruction wrought by dissention between partners, beginning with just such trifles as this. He hated bickering and sought to avoid it as a rattlesnake in the grass.

Aleck had cooked a noonday meal but had eaten most of it so the returned hunter was obliged to cook also. He cut and fried steak and when he ate, Aleck ate again. Jim suggested that they start on the return journey that afternoon and Stern sulkily agreed. After dinner, Dark Jim ascended the cliff wall and silently tried to repair the damage his partner had done. Stern watched him suspiciously, but saw no sign that indicated knowledge of the small theft. When Dark Jim descended they packed the two little burros, turned their heads down the canyon, and started for civilization.

Only three days had gone by when they returned to the cave. Although insufficient time had elapsed for the trip to the nearest town, there returned with them a third man and three additional burros, loaded with provisions and mining implements. This man evidently of Dutch origin, went by the name of "Steinie." He was short and fat, around fifty years old, with a round fat face and gray eyes, deep-set and weak-looking behind gold-rimmed spectacles. He spoke with a European accent, but his skin was ivory-tinted, his hair dark brown and straight, and a close-cropped dark brown mustache was on his upper lip.

His appearance as a whole, including his earnest way of speaking, gave an impression of practicality and efficiency, and it was this impression that had prevailed on the two prospectors to return with him to the discovery. He had argued, earnestly insistent, that Dark Jim had neglected to investigate what probably would be the richest part of the discovery: the placer at the base of the cliff. He pointed out that if there was much gold in the rock of the bluff then there must be also a great deal loose in the sand at its base. No mining company would be necssary to exploit this placer, and earnestly proclaiming himself as one of the best placer miners in the West, he implored them to return and let him show how to work it most efficiently. He had the tools on his burros.

Aleck Stern, much impressed by the man's argument, insisted that they return; and in the end Dark Jim, outnumbered, yielded.

"Well, what do you think of it?" Dark Jim asked after showing the Dutchman the prospect.

"Very goot — very goot, indeedt. Put I pelieve you vass right about dat mining companee. Dat cliff iss pig and it would be petter vorked vid uh pig companee. Yass." The Dutchman sucked in his breath and continued talking. "Ya-as. Ug pig companee could vork on uh pig scale an' take down dah whole cliff, Py Gott! Dat vould mean pig money for us all!"

"Well, ain't that just what I told you? Didn't I tell you the size of the cliff and everything? And you said the placer was our best bet, didn't you?"

"Ya-as, put dah placer iss nutting — nutting, Dark Jim — compared to dat cliff."

Jim thought, I notice you're not making any great effort toward scaling the cliff to judge it right. Probably you don't want to placer and don't want to climb because you're too damned lazy. Reckon that's the reason you're so fat. But he said only, "Well, I have most of the cliff staked off, four claims,"

"Yes," chimed in Aleck Stern, belligerently, "and we ain't got enough staked off at that."

The Dutchman fingered his mustache thoughtfully and went into the cave to prepare something to eat. The only thing in the world that he liked better than good food he said, was good beer; he was a connoisseur of beer, but had none now. Aleck Stern followed, his long, blackish mustache bristling with anger. There was dynamite in the air. And Dark Jim, perceiving it, took his prospecting hammer, went out and did some more work on the cliff.

He worked late, a busy bee while the drones sat in the cave and amused themselves. When he came in he found the Dutchman on one side of the cave reading a newspaper he had brought while Aleck sat on the other side busily, but somewhat unmusically twanging his Jew's-harp, and all the while warily watching the Dutchman.

Seeing that the others had used up all the wood in the cave, Jim went back out, collected an armful and returned. The sun had gone down, a ball of fire behind a distant peak, and, as always in the high, dry air, the temperature dropped rapidly with its setting. He built a good fire at the mouth of the cave and the interior was soon ablaze with its light.

Then he proceeded to cook supper, as the others had left him very little from their meal. He filled the coffee pot and put it on the fire, made bread in the dutch oven, fried steak in a skillet, then opened and warmed a can of chile con carne, and sat down on the earthen floor to eat. He ate slowly, as was his custom, and then unhurriedly washed the dishes. After which, sitting down again on the cave floor, he took his old pipe from his trousers, slowly filled it, and carefully tamped the tobacco in the bowl. The upper rim of the bowl was slightly chipped away, as if broken by one of the boulders that had played so important a part in his life. He could not remember how many years that old pipe had served him faithfully, through fair weather and foul. Short, wild months of good fortune, and long, dismal hard-luck years. He always handled it with slow, loving hands, and made a rite of filling it and tamping the tobacco in place.

He smoked meditatively, and studied the faces of his two companions. Steinie, the Dutchman, by the aid of the flickering light of the fire, still read the newspaper, while Aleck Stern sat, with his back and the butts of his two revolvers towards Dark Jim, still twanging the Jew's-harp, and occasionally casting black glances at the fat back of the suave Dutchman. What a disagreeable pair, Dark Jim thought. Neither will work; each is very selfish; each wants something for nothing. Aleck Stern was bad enough, but now the bitter pill is doubled. Never before have I had such bad luck choosing partners. Ah well, that's life. Bitter with the sweet, the bitter seldom in single doses; misfortune coming with good fortune. Like gold and dross, old Jim. The dross has to be separated. And cast out!

But one need not sit with hands folded; one could at least endeavor to separate the two, to remove the bitter from the sweet, the dross from the gold. After all, he, alone and unaided, had found this mine, and had done all the work connected with it. Aleck Stern had done nothing but sign his name to the papers in the monuments, the Dutchman nothing at all.

He removed his pipe. "Listen, men. We're getting short of meat again. What you say one of you come with me in the morning and we'll get the rest of that steer I killed. It'll keep in this weather. We'll take two burros and maybe get a deer on the way."

"I don't think I ought to go," said Aleck Stern. "One of us oughta stay here and watch our mine." He said "our" with emphasis.

The Dutchman said: "I think dat iss uh goot idea, Aleck. I tink it iss — only, two men iss needed, one to vatch dah one dat vatches. Yaas. So, I tink I stay too. You take dah burro, Dark Jim, and get dah beef. One man iss enough I tink."

Jim did not argue. When the time comes I'll fight, if necessary; but I will not argue, he thought.

The Dutchman read a while longer, then folded up his newspaper, spread out his bedding in the back of the cave and turned in. Soon he was followed by Aleck Stern, who as was his custom, carefully placed both revolvers beneath his pillow. Aleck Stern was never seen without those two pistols. And two rifles lay between him and the cave wall. Presently both were asleep, Aleck snoring raucously, and Dark Jim sat on, while the fire burned low. Brooding on life, gold, and his surly companions.

The following morning Jim left with his burro at break of day Making better time than before, he returned with the beef some two hours before noon. Leaving the burro some distance up the canyon, he stealthily approached the cave on foot, hardly knowing what he expected to see. But it was the same scene as the last time he had returned alone: the Dutchman nowhere to be seen, and Aleck Stern, halfway up the bluff collecting gold in his tobacco pouch. Dark Jim felt himself nearly berserk with rage. But he strove to control himself. He walked forward, apparently his usual calm self except that his dusky face looked ashen and sinister. On seeing him, Aleck dropped the pouch in his pocket, and went on hammering at a stone. Then he looked down and, as if seeing Jim for the first time, nervously descended.

"Thought I'd work a little," he explained agitatedly.

"Where's the Dutchman?" asked Dark Jim in a level, impersonal voice.

"Gone to look for one of his burros. Cussed you out for taking it, but I says you didn't. Say, what do you think that damned skunk did this morning while I was asleep? He put his name *above* ours on all the monument papers, just like he helped find this mine. You gonna let him git away with that? I ain't, I tell you! I ain't gonna stand for it *no* longer!" His voice had become loud and uglied with anger.

"Come with me. I got something to tell you," said Dark Jim, ominously calm.

He led the way, and Aleck, with a frown followed up the canyon, and around a bend, where the two sat down on a boulder.

Dark Jim waited a moment. "Now then," he began slowly and ominously, "this Dutchman's here with us. There's only *one* way we can get rid of him. *Kill him and stow him in a cliff!*"

Aleck Stern jumped as if shot and spread his hands before his face as if to ward off a blow. "Not that, Dark Jim, not *that!*"

"No, you low-life hound, I knew it. You ain't got the nerve to do it! That's the reason you sleep on your guns — you got no nerve and you try to bluff with your guns." Jim's voice became savage. "Now listen here! Not an ounce of that gold in that mine there is yours — not a damned ounce! I found it after you'd quit me. Another thing — I've caught you stealing my gold *twice.* Now you take that gold — and your tobacco sacks and your stuff — and your burro — and get the hell out of the this camp! I'll give you thirty minutes! Leave behind one of your rifles to pay for that gold. You ain't got the nerve to use it and I have. Now — get!" Dark Jim punctuated his last sentence with a shot from his revolver. The bullet grazed the other's arm.

Stern, his face ashen with fear, anxiously looked at Dark Jim. An awful, implacable malice had come into that dark face. Reminiscent of the tales that had been said of Dark Jim when he was young. Tales from out in the silent spaces. Rumors, exaggerated perhaps, but, where there's smoke there's fire.

"Get!" Dark Jim repeated, "get out of my sight or I will kill you."

Extremely frightened by what he saw in Dark Jim's face and the cocked revolver ready in his hand, Stern said, "You *would!* You're as mean as your face. Don't shoot! I'll go!"

Stern hurried away. Dark Jim, revolver still in hand, followed him to the cave.

He hurriedly packed, and shortly was gone. Carrying with him all his possessions but one rifle, which lay on the cave floor.

Presently the Dutchman came over the brow of a nearby hill and hurried to the cave. With an axe, Dark Jim was cutting off a green mesquite limb, on which to hang the beef that was still loaded on his burro.

"Where iss Stern?" asked the Dutchman.

"Decided to leave all of a sudden."

"Dat's queer. Do you know why he leave?"

Dark Jim gave a hard hack at the limb, and it fell at his feet. He did not answer, it was as though he had not heard. His face was calm, immobile like a piece of dark, sculptured stone. The Dutchman noted again the dark cast of those features, and thought he saw something sinister there — something that gripped his heart with a cold clammy fear. Dark Jim, his name was; and he had been named right. Black he was and looked capable of black deeds of violence. Why had he not marked this enough before? Because of the man's silence and calm? Yes, he was silent, and calm, and sure! Like a viper! He did not argue before he struck. Aleck Stern with all his reckless defiance and bravado compared to this man had been a mere noisy boy. And he had not seen this clearly before; well, he saw it now. Danger lay in the direction of Dark Jim.

He returned to the cave, convinced in his own mind that Dark Jim had done away with Aleck Stern; when he had left Aleck had been in camp, when he returned Aleck was gone. In the interim he had heard a shot; therefore, the man had been murdered. When he saw one of Aleck's beloved rifles lying on the floor of the cave, his conviction became certainty; and he knew with a sick feeling of fear, that henceforth he was doomed to be constantly on the alert.

With his gun, Dark Jim had come in. It was holstered now; but the Dutchman watched his every move. Like a hunted animal at bay.

Jim started a fire and began making preparations to cook. To his surprise, the Dutchman did likewise.

"I you want any steak go out and cut yourself some," said Dark Jim. "I don't want any."

At the mention of steak, the rotund little man hungrily took a butcher knife and went out to the tree where the beef hung. He was busily cutting away, when he noticed something about the meat that made him spring back in horror, knife in hand. The black work had already begun. The beef was poisoned! Its surface was covered with tiny swellings, protruberances that resembled blisters. Shaken, he returned to the cave.

Black Jim looked up from his work unconcernedly. "Where's your steak?"

"I tink I don't vant any," replied the other agitatedly. "I am not hungry."

That night the Dutchman did not retire so early but waited until long after Dark Jim was in bed and asleep. When at length he did turn in, placing his revolver in easy reach of his hand, he could not sleep. All that night he dozed fitfully, harassed by a terrible nightmare, wherein Dark Jim, long, wicked knife in hand, pursued him to the edge of a precipice where he was forced to either jump over or return and be run through with the knife. Always he woke to clutch his revolver frantically, sit bolt upright and stare wide-eyed toward the rear of the cave where Dark Jim slept. He spent a miserable night and the following morning looked haggard.

The next night was a repetition of the night before and on the third day he was so nervous that he started at the slightest sound and occasionally had a violent shudder, like the vibration of a snapped spring. At noon while he was reopening a can of fish that he had opened the night before, he was so nervous that he cut his right forefinger on the tin. Not wanting Dark Jim to recognize his weakness he sidled out of the tent, hiding the cut finger and watching the other out of the corner of his eye. Dark Jim was in his eye continually now; and his revolver never out of his reach. He began to realize why Aleck

Stern had always worn his guns.

When he returned with the flow of blood staunched, Dark Jim was mixing dough. Working mostly with his left hand, the Dutchman took fish from the can, finished preparing his meal, and sat down on the dirt floor to eat.

In the midst of his meal, he sprang to his feet, a wild light in his eyes, and he yelled: "You poisoned me! You poisoned dah beef — you poisoned dis sardine! You murderer!" Retching, he looked wildly about the cave.

His eyes fell on the coal-oil can. He snatched it up and gulped down some of its contents from the spout. The kerosene acted as a rapid and efficient emetic. No sooner was he relieved than he ran wildly out of the cave. He turned for a moment to shoot twice at the entrance, and fled up the canyon to where one of his burros stood, tied and packed for just such an emergency. He heard shots from the vicinity of the cave, and frantically untied the little animal and drove him out of the canyon, every step cursing and beating him with a mesquite limb.

With smoking revolver, Jim turned back into the cave. He curiously inspected the food the other had been eating, fish, old and of inferior quality. He thought of its can that had stood overnight opened, with the fish still in it. He tasted it, and half-smiled: "No ptomaine poison here. Just nervous."

He went out to cut a piece of meat, and noted the little protruberances on it and mused, "Funny how those sun blisters come on meat out in the open. I figgered the Dutchman was too much of a tenderfoot to know about that. I figgered he'd think I poisoned it." He half-smiled sardonically. Good riddance to both of them. After all, my dark skin is worth something to me.

"I'm through," he muttered. "Through with partners!"

He took his shovel and placer pan and went down to the base of the precipice, just below the cave of gold.

He dug into the hollowed out bowl at that base and filled the pan with placer gold, gravel and sand. Adding water, he shook the pan with a continual rotary and reciprocal motion, spilling the gravel and dirt over its edge. When he was through, he looked at its bottom with satisfaction. Just as he had expected; the pan-bottom was literally lined with gold. Taking from his pocket a wide mouthed bottle full of mercury, he poured some of it into the pan. Then he took the amalgam thus formed, and put it into his old prospector's chamois-

36

skin bag, and gently squeezed the bag over the bottle. The mercury oozed out through the pores of the skin.

The gold was inside the bag; he threw the remaining sand and gravel from the pan and looked in the bag. There it was in the Arizona sunshine, clean of dirt, oil of human life's wheels taken from its attendant refuse. He had retained the gold; and he had got rid of the dross.

"So, Morton," he said, ending his story, to me, "that is why I never had another partner."

"Jim, I see no evidence of wealth in your outfit. What happened to your gold?"

Dark Jim smiled his peculiar half-smile. "I spent it all. On wild women, gambling, and gifts to people. For two years I lived high on the hog. And the placer played out. And next the gold vein came to an end. That's the way gold is, uncertain."

"I still believe you need a companion out there. What'd happen to you if you got terribly sick?"

"I'd get well — or I'd die. No, I'll have no other partners. I don't belong with them. They don't belong with me. You see, Morton, I am not what you call a 'civilized' man. I belong out there. In the Great Lonesome."

CHAPTER 3
Guns at Patagonia

My new friend of the Nogales Immigration Office, Immigration Inspector Hugh Walker, was with me when quite an adventure occurred near our Patagonia Border Patrol Station. Hugh Walker was a native of Arkansas, a cocky little fellow who talked a lot about his remarkable adventures of the past. Some of his stories were almost incredible, but his quite evident sincerity made me believe them. For I knew he wouldn't be lying about his military record. Considerably older than I, he was eighteen when war broke out in Europe. And, before the United States entered it, he rushed to Canada to volunteer. He was short and of small weight so he was a natural for aviation training. In 1916 he went into the Lafayette Escadrille as an aviator in France, flying the open-cockpit little planes of the time. Just flying them was danger enough, but in addition there were the aerial dogfights, trying to kill your opponent before you yourself were shot down in flames. Talk about the gladiators of ancient Rome! They probably had less danger in their lives than had Hugh and his comrades-in-arms, including Quentin Roosevelt, son of President Theodore Roosevelt, who died fighting in the Lafayette Escadrille. Oh, Hugh had met the test of courage all right. And he was to meet it again on a lesser scale that Saturday afternoon standing by my side while I stopped traffic, and checked motor vehicles and passengers at the Border Patrol station. He had no responsibility to help me, but he enjoyed the work, the possibility of danger in it. He was in his immigration uniform; and the presence of another armed officer there added to the impression of dignified authority at the checkpoint. He also helped by holding one end of our stop sign across the road, and in the usually brief inspection.

After an hour or so of this a car came that did not stop. It knocked our canvas stop sign out of our hands, and kept on going! I saw that the driver was a middle-aged man with a ruddy face, a North American or from some country in North Europe. The person by his side obviously was quite young, a mere girl with a smooth, ivory complexion, looing like the patrician girls I had known in Spain.

Hugh and I hopped into my nearby car, and we started after them at high speed. We seemed to be very slowly gaining on them, when Hugh whipped his automatic from its holster, and began firing at their tires. Without success, he emptied the gun, then reloaded.

Then, to our surprise, the car ahead slowed, and stopped. We got out and with drawn guns hopped on opposite sides of the running boards. Both of the passengers had their hands up. We took the man's gun, and ordered them out.

Hugh was inspecting the car and I was frisking the man when I felt a pistol come up against my back.

"Let me have your gun," the girl said in good English, "or I kill you!"

Well, what could I do? There's nothing more disconcerting than a cold steel muzzle against your back.

"Turn slow," she said. And as I did what she ordered she slowly turned with me still keeping that damned gun against my back. Another feminine-voiced order came: "Hold your gun by the barrel, and hand it to me." Again I followed orders. She was only a girl but she had that little pistol cocked. And I was afraid she was nervous.

From the car Hugh saw the situation. He turned, and said to the man: "Get in the car." With alacrity, he obeyed.

"Get back in the car, honey," I said. "We have to let you go. I don't know where or why you're going, but I believe you're making a terrible mistake."

She prodded me with that cocked gun and I moved ahead of her to the car. The man had already demanded and received his gun back. He had started the engine, and the door was open for her. With the gun still on me she cautiously got in. Then, being no robber, she threw my gun on the ground. But I had no time to use it. For, with the engine roaring, they were gone.

"We lost that round, Hugh," I said. "But we'll catch up with them."

Back in my car, we were after them in short order. Well, it was another engine-roaring, desperate chase, bouncing through the drainage ditches across the road, slowly gaining on them. Again Hugh was leaning out and firing. This time his sixth bullet hit the mark. Their right rear tire went flat and the car ahead careened and weaved to a stop.

With our guns cocked, Hugh went to the driver and I again to the girl. We were faced by both of their guns. But this time I was trying to take no chances on that innocent-looking but dangerous girl. I ran to her side. But before I could get to her she began firing. Fortunately, her two shots missed me. Then I shot her. I shot her in the right shoulder. And apparently I broke it, for her little gun dropped to the car floor. Then I thought: Dear God, I have shot a woman! And I'm sorry.

But I grabbed her by her left arm and as gently as possible in view of her screaming and kicking, forced her out of the car.

"You're under arrest," I said, "for attacking a U.S. officer."

I forcibly held her in my arms a moment and inspected her wound. It was bleeding but not badly. After looking at the back of her shoulder, I realized my bullet had gone on through.

Then readying again my pistol, I turned my attention to Hugh and the man. Quickly, I realized there was nothing I could do to help Hugh out of a desperate situation. The man was on his feet and his gun was pointed at Hugh's heart. And at the same time Hugh had his cocked gun pointed at his adversary's chest. Their eyes were glaring at each other. I knew that if I shot his opponent the next moment Hugh would be dead.

For a moment that seemed an eternity they stood there, guns of death aimed and cocked, the sensuous-faced, cruel-looking, big light-haired man; and the wiry little World War I aviator, my friend Hugh. I felt he would never back down, for the same brave spirit that had been with him in those terrible aerial duels in northern France was there.

And as he had done in the European battlefront, so did he here. He won! The big man dropped his gun and put up his hands. Again my friend Hugh was a survivor!

I closed the station and took the wounded girl, who would give us only her first name of Esmeralda, to the only doctor near that I knew, a veterinarian whom we called Doc Carver. The doctor treated and bound her wound. Then I set out for the Nogales Immigration Office, taking the girl separately there, while Hugh took the man under guard by his side, and his wife Bobby rode in the back seat. Thus we made sure our two prisoners couldn't talk with each other during the trip.

At the Immigration Office we learned that I had correctly appraised the nature of the girl's background. She was from an aristocratic family. Her father was a judge. Since learning that his sixteen-year-old daughter was missing — presumably kidnapped by a "light-complected *gringo*," he had made the wires hot to Nogales, Sonora; and the *Oficina de Inmigración* there had relayed the situation to our side of the line.

As for the man, we learned that he was an American, a convicted white slaver, escaped from prison, a holder of a false passport.

With the duped little Esmeralda, he was driving to Nevada. There he and a pimp forcibly and repeatedly would have broken the poor girl into promiscuous sex. And then, after a week or so, ashamed and forlorn, she would have been put in a house of prostitution of the worst type.

On recommendations of myself and Hugh, Esmeralda was returned by the U.S. Immigration Office to the Oficina de Inmigración of Nogales, Sonora and thence to the supervison and protection of her father.

"Richard, where have you been?" my wife Laura said. "I've been worried."

I said, "I hoped you wouldn't know I was gone." Then, not wanting to disturb her further, I told her very briefly about my afternoon.

But she was not satisfied with the details, for later: "Richard, I know something bad has happened to you today. I can tell how you feel."

"Well, Laura, for the first time in my life I have physically hurt a woman — a young lady — a girl. In fact, I shot her. But fortuntely, I didn't kill her." And I told Laura the whole story.

CHAPTER 4
Sometimes the Law Is An Ass

Lou Quinn came on brief duty at our Patagonia Border Patrol Station. You might say that Lou was a man from the past. Middle-aged, a veteran cowboy and ranch owner and the only man I have ever known in the old days who had been on a trail-herd drive to the old railhead in Kansas. He was tall, square and well-built, not wiry like Zane Grey's western heroes but nevertheless stuff that romances have been made of. A quiet, soft-spoken man of Texas origin, a good horseman and marksman, he seemed to belong, not indoors, but to the wild, open spaces that still were with us in southern Arizona, but were slowly passing.

He was there to select men to be with him on duty in the Nogales area. He chose two. I was proud to be one he wanted. The other was Lawrence Sipe.

The three of us reported for duty in Nogales. Lou was in charge, but Lawrence and I mostly were on our own. We were to scout up and down the line, and on the roads that went northward from Nogales, one via Patagonia, the other via the sparse settlement of Tubac and the ruins of Father Kino's old Spanish Mission there.

I was fascinated by Nogales in Arizona and the larger town of Nogales, Sonora, Mexico with the short-distance barbed wire fence that extended on each side of the Gates or *Garitas*, the smuggler's holes in that fence, and the cactus-studded, mountainous country strangely appealing in the bright sunshine and the clear air like wine. There were two *Garitas* on each side of the line, one at Morely Avenue, the other at Grand Avenue. I came to know customs Inspector Houston, a former Marine, who sometimes Texas-drawled with a deadly look. One day I heard him say to an irritated, sharp-speaking, line-crossing woman: "Don't-t- *speak* to me—like that! I *ain't* used to it!" The woman eased her vitrolic tongue. And there was old Mr. Roberts, an

Agricultural Inspector and an Immigration Inspector named O'Toole. And I was much interested in the sometimes colorful, sometimes pitiful people to the south of us who legally came through the *Garitas* each day into *la tierra de los Yanquis*. A healthy young man such as myself cannot help having the normal feelings of young manhood; and sometimes I was romantically stirred by the mysterious soft femininity of the dark-eyed *señoritas* who came through those gates. We like or love our opposites and those dark-eyed, softly feminine little women from the romantic, archaic land of Old Mexico were my opposites. They fascinated me.

One day it was my fate to find one who was utterly feminine and attractive to me and yet not soft.

In the green uniform of the U.S. Border Patrol, wearing the regulation wide-brimmed hat and a revolver at my side, I was driving on the northern edge of the little border town when I saw her. She looked like a Mexican-American girl who might be living on the street where she was walking. But by this time I seemed to have developed a sixth sense for detecting the presence of an illegally-entered alien or smuggler; and there was something about her, perhaps a tense uneasiness, that caused me to think she might be "wet." So I stopped my car and spoke to her.

She turned a frightened, frustrated glance at me. But her dark eyes quickly seemed to flash fire when I asked: "*Tiene papeles de Inmigracion?*"

As long as I live I'll never forget her look in reaction. It was not at all submissive as most questioned aliens were, but *utterly* defiant. She stamped her little foot and cried: "Speak to me in English! I am not a Mexican. I am an *American!*"

"All right. Do you have Immigration papers?"

Again she stamped her foot, and she spat out: "No! Oh, how I *hate* you Immigration!"

How very beautiful! I thought. Brown eyes, sparkling with anger, and small, beautifully shaped, very feminine body. Young, fiery maturity! I could surely go for that girl!

But I was on duty so I asked: "Do you have proof of your birth here?"

"No. I was born in Mexico. My mother and father died and I went to Los Angeles as a baby. My aunt raised me. She's dead now."

"Are you coming from Mexico now?"

"Yes. I went to look for my relatives. The few that I found are poor — poor! So I'm coming back to my home in Los Angeles."

"Anybody there to take of you?"

"No! *I'll* take care of myself. I can work."

"Do you have enough money to insure you won't be a public charge?"

"No. But I *said* I'll work."

I thought, she doesn't say "Sir" or "Señor." What an independent girl!

"I'm sorry," I said, "but I need to take you to the Immigration Office."

She resisted, and I picked her up and physically forced her into the car. The touch of her feminine body was very attractive to me.

At the office, Immigration Inspector Blea took charge of her case; and I learned her aristocratic name: Victoria Talavera de Toledo. He found she had a record there — had applied for admittance; been held for the Board of Special Inquiry; and was denied on our frequent catchall ground — as "a person likely to become a public charge." There was nothing else against her, only poverty. I was not surprised that the Inspector who originally had considered her application was the one we called "Mac" — short for McGuire, well-liked by the Immigration force, but with a reputation for being hard in examinations of aliens. Some other inspector, who perhaps had too much compassion for the job like myself, I felt sometimes, might have admitted her.

Inspector Blea, a swarthy, stocky, middle-aged Mexican-American, first spoke to her in Spanish; and amusedly I suspected how she would react. I was not surprised, for quickly, angrily, she dressed him down about talking to her in her own language — English. Then Blea, who never seemed perturbed by anything, calmly told her in English the bad news: that she had to go back across the line. To Nogales, Sonora.

"But," she cried indignantly, "*how* am I going to *live* over there?"

Blea shurgged. "*Quien sabe?* Who knows. There are thousands of people there. They live, somehow."

So, my poor little beauty Victoria was to be conducted to the Gate or *Garita*, and figuratively shoved out of the country. It was the job of the Immigration Guard, a quiet, pale-faced, earnest man named Preston. But he agreed to let me take her to the *Garita*.

Before crossing the line, I asked her to stop a moment. And I said: "Victoria, you may not believe me, but I'm really very sorry about what's happened to you. I see your record before the Boards isn't really bad. But all the money you had was just enough to pay your head-tax and, by starving yourself, pay your bus fare to Los Angeles. Then the Board wondered what you'd do. And you, frankly, honestly, said you were no longer a *señorita*, but a *señora*. So, with some sort of sexual relation in the past, they thought you might turn to prostitution."

"A prostitute!" she spat out the word. "They're crazy! Victoria Talavera de Toledo is no prostitute. I would *work!*"

"I believe you. But the Board didn't know that. The law's the law, Victoria. I am sorry; but I just did my duty. Now, I suggest you get a job across the line, save your money, and when you get enough to make sure you won't need to turn to charity or be jailed, try again."

"Hah!" she scorned. "The jobs over there wouldn't pay me enough to *live!* much less to *save.* And I would *not* be a prostitute!"

She spoke bitterly. So very outspoken, I thought. And so very beautiful!

"Well, Victoria," I said, "let's get it over with." And we walked to the Mexican side.

I thought then I was through with the trauma of dealing with the fiery little Victoria. But definitely I was not.

Coming back to the American side, I stopped to talk a little while with the wise old U.S. Agriculture Inspector on duty, checking for barred disease-carrying Mexican fruit and vegetables. Medium-sized, gray-haired, his name was Roberts; and he was nearing retirement after many years of service.

"A pretty girl you took across the line, Morton," he said. "What was wrong with her?"

"She was barred by the Board of Special Inquiry. Mac should have admitted her in the first place. But when you get any case in the hands of a committee or board they're usually going to be hard and red-tapish. The main thing against her was just poverty, no parents, uncles or aunts in L.A. But she didn't lie to 'em, told 'em frankly, she was an unmarried *señora* — instead of a *señorita*."

"So what, Richard! That doesn't make her a prostitute."

"It certainly does not, not even a mistress. She said she had never lived in concubinage. And she gets fighting-angry at the mention of her turning to prostitution. You ought to see her when she's *really angry!* A beautiful girl, Mr. Roberts. Beautiful and fiery. And in a fight for her life."

"Too bad. The law isn't always right, you know. It's made for the average, not the individual. Charles Dickens had a fictional character who had a point. He said: 'The law is an ass!' Sometimes, I've learned, the law really is an ass! A big, bumbling jackass. And so are we who enforce it. *Sometimes*. If that be treason," he smiled, "so be it."

I returned to the Immigration Office, and there was accosted by a Border Patrol Inspector with the surname of Harvey. He was married, older than I, and seemed to be about middle age. "Morton," he said, "that was *some* beauty you took across the line."

His shifty brown eyes slithered to the side, and with an amused smile he added: "You ought've taken her up a canyon, had sex with her, and let her off far up the road to the north."

"Man! You *must* be joking. I'd have been derelict in my duty. But I will say one thing, she should not have been barred in the first place."

His eyes shifted again. "You *must* have been attracted to her."

"Sure. Of course, Harvey."

It was only the next day, when I was scouting, using my own automobile as we frequently did for the low-budgeted Border Patrol, on the northern, wild and barren environs of the town, when it was my fate again to overtake Victoria Talavera de Toledo.

At first, as before, she faced me defiantly, like a little trapped animal desperately rearing up against the trapper. But then, probably thinking that such anger harmed her case with the powerful immigration officers, she controlled her anger and changed her tune, becoming seemingly submissive, but pleading. I had liked her better in her frank defiance. Nevertheless, I was thrilled and attracted by what she next said: "*Señor*, you like me, no?"

"Yes, Victoria. I definitely do."

I realized that she probably appreciated my having been kind to her at the line; but I knew she must be acting as she stared at me with seeming passion in the dark mystery of those brown eyes. It was the utterly feminine come-hither look that doubtless went back to the Stone Age of early man. Such a look as Eve with an apple in her hand might have had for Adam in the beginning of our time.

Oh, how I was vulnerable! But I wondered, somewhat uneasily, if any other Patrol Inspectors would soon scout this way north of Nogales. I thought not, as this was part of my territory for this shift.

It seemed it would be *so* easy to pick her up and drive northward instead of duty-bound southward to the Immigration Office. I thought, I have been highly attentive to duty all my life. can't I have just one fling?

Then her next words all the more stirred up my masculine, tending-to-wander nature: "Señor I'll deny you nothing. If you'll only drive me up a way toward Tucson." She was still magnetically staring at me with passion, or simulated passion.

I was strongly confronted by conflicting emotions: adherence to my long-standing mores of duty, to my governmental employment and to my wife, or for once having a natural breakaway of male escape from the rigid conventions of my youth into freedom and variety in sex.

Thus I stood there a moment, debating, with the sands of time and fate running out, and the beautiful, sexy girl waiting, with that seemingly passionate, come-hither look. Then I spoke: "How much money do you have, Victoria?"

"Not much, Sir. I spent part of it to live in Sonora last night. Only about twelve dollars left. And Señor, I'll give all of it to you, and also myself, to just drive me northward a ways. Just twenty miles, Señor."

"Victoria, my dear, we ought to face the consequences squarely before we go any further into this proposition. Attractive though it is. I of course don't want your money at all. That would be a bribe, and if I was caught, the loss of my job and a prison sentence for both of us. And your other offer of sex is also a bribe."

"But, Sir, wouldn't it be worth the chance? To both of us. Have you ever had sex on the ground? I haven't. But, you know, it might be very enjoyable." She smiled in invitation.

"Get in the car!" I suddenly ordered. She obeyed. And then I began driving fast, northward. Toward Tucson, but not via Patagonia, where we had a Border Patrol Station and checkpoint. Toward Tubac over the frequently free-of-officers road that way. A mile or so short of Tubac, I stopped the car.

"Victoria, are you a Catholic?"

"Yes, Sir."

"I'm not. I'm a Protestant. But our God is the same. Are you willing to swear, before God, that you'll never tell anyone that I helped you escape toward Tucson?"

"Oh, yes, Sir!"

I had her hold up her right hand and gave her the oath as though she were in court. Then she crossed herself.

We kissed, long and passionately. "This is goodbye for us," I said.

Still in my arms, puzzled, she looked inquiringly at me. I took a ten-dollar bill from my pocket, money I could hardly afford to give; handing it to her I said, "Victoria, you've really given me a thrill. But it's not in me to accept *any* bribe. And I strongly suggest to you, my beautiful one, don't *ever* again offer such a bribe to any American-side officer. He might arrest you for it."

Seemingly shocked, she sat there a moment more in my arms. Then, impulsively, she kissed me and said, "Sir, I *am* sorry. I was badly wrong about you. You are a *good, good* person! And I thank you from the depth of my heart."

"*No hay de que*," I said, and then hastily translated, "It is nothing."

"But it is, my fine *Señor*."

"Now," I continued, "this road northward goes on to Tucson. There'll be more traffic on it in about an hour. So a while before sunset, stop walking on it, and pick it up again at night. The moon will be up, nearly full. At Tubac you'll see an old Spanish Mission. Very near it a Mexican and his wife live in an *adobe* hut. We have never received any information from them so they *might* be safe for you to stay there tonight. But it would be better to get a *very good* drink of water from his well, and keep on hiking northward. It's a long, long walk, about forty-five miles! Don't board any bus and don't hitch-hike until you're in Tucson. From there take the bus to Los Angeles, but not by Yuma, it's too near the border. Go by Phoenix and Blythe. You have two strikes against you but I do hope you make it. Go with God."

She kissed me goodbye, got out, and began walking. A forlorn, beautiful little woman. My heart went out to her: a Spanish-American waif longing for return to southern California, in the country we conquered from her ancestors.

I returned to Nogales, parked my car well east of the town and spent the rest of my day's watch scouting on foot, sometimes hidden along trails frequently used by smugglers and illegally entering aliens. I saw none, and so at length returned to the Immigration Office.

I had written out my day's report, of course avoiding reference to Victoria, when a beefy, red-faced Patrol Inspector named Brian Watts approached me, "Morton, a tip just came over the telephone. An illegal alien walking north of Tubac. Nervous, frightened.

Obviously 'wet'. Do you want to drive up there with me?"

Uneasy, I asked, "What kind of alien, a smuggler?"

"No. A young woman, very pretty, the informant said."

I thought, poor, poor Victoria. And poor me, if she breaks her oath under hard questioning.

"No, Brian," I answered. "Just a woman. You can handle that alone. I've had enough scouting for today."

That night in bed I was restless, so restless that my wife, with her usual keen sensitivity to the feelings of others and especially myself said, "Richard, *what* is it that's bothering you?"

"Oh, an immigration case. No need to talk about it. Let's get to sleep." I feigned slumber and at last slept.

The next day I got the file of Victoria's second "voluntary return" to Mexico, to avoid prison and red-tape deportation. She had kept her word and had not mentioned my name. I breathed more easily.

Well, I thought again that my dealings with the fiery and lovable little Victoria were of the past but again I was mistaken. I was at the Grand Avenue Gate one day when who should approach me from the Mexican side but Victoria Talavera de Toledo! She was obviously pregnant.

"Hello, Victoria," I said.

"Hello, Sir," she replied in a low, subdued voice. And she handed me a typed note.

It read: "Please let Victoria Talavera de Toledo go to the Immigration Office to see about getting a local crossing card to shop in Nogales, Arizona." It was signed with a Mexican woman's name. I looked at this pitiful note and an overwhelming sadness came over me. I saw that it had become very soiled with usage, so much so that I knew it was a subterfuge. She was not going to the Immigration Office, for she knew it would be useless. She was using this soiled note only for her scanty shopping on the U.S. side.

I handed the note to the Immigration Inspector on duty there, Jerry O'Toole. He looked at it a moment, then handed it back to Victoria. "*Pase*," he said. "Go ahead."

After she had left, O'Toole turned to me: "I know that girl isn't going to the Office. She just wants to shop. No harm to anybody. When she comes while I'm on duty I don't send her under guard. I just let her through. She always comes back by me here. Poor little kid! She's pregnant, she's not going anywhere."

Agricultural Inspector Roberts happened to be on duty at the same time O'Toole was that day. Looking at me, he asked, "Wasn't that the girl you put across the line some time ago?"

"Yes, Mr. Roberts. The same."

"She doesn't look as pretty as she did."

"No wonder. Beaten down by her life. Frustrated. Pregnant. She has lost her fire, Mr. Roberts. And her defiant fire was part of her beauty."

"Too bad," the kind old man said. "We all lose our fire of youth. But her loss has come too young, and too suddenly. I'm sorry."

"Probably not as sorry as I am. Her life has become like an ancient-Greek tragedy. I remember what you said about the quotation from Dickens, that the law is an ass. That's extreme, of course, Mr. Roberts. Mostly our law enforcement is fair. Often hard, but just. But sometimes the law really *is* a stupid ass. A monstrous, red-taped, braying jackass!"

CHAPTER 5
Contraband Love

Lawrence Sipe and I sat in a car parked in a rocky canyon. Behind us the black shapes of clumps of mesquite intensified the darkness; and in front we could see the vague outlines of a small concrete railway bridge. Overhead, in the Arizona skies, millions of stars twinkled coldly, and in the west hung a thin wisp of a moon. It was about two a.m.

Lawrence coughed. He knew there were no smugglers then in that area; yet, out of habit, he cupped his hands over his mouth muffling the sound. "This," he remarked, "would be a hell of a job for a T.B. He'd die right off the bat, with a bullet in his head."

"Yes, or a cigarette fiend. I've known some that coughed worse than T.B.'s." Restlessly, I shifted my position. "I wish that train would come on! I'm getting tired of lying out here every night with nothing happening. I joined this outfit for adventure. And I've found some. But this certainly is no example of it."

"Adventure!" Sipe scoffed. "You're younger than I am. I had too much of what you'd call adventure in the war. I remember those cockeyed rains of northern France. Rains! Rains! Muddy trenches! 'Over the top, boys!' Shoot 'em! Kill 'em with the bayonet!' You can call it adventure. I call it plain hell!"

"I guess it was. But it's different here. We just occasionally get in a gunfight. And when you make an arrest you're learning about other people. And earning your pay."

"The pay's the only thing I'm in this for. I got my hand in Uncle Sam's pocket and I ain't never gonna take it out."

"That's a pretty cavalier approach, Lawrence."

"Just kidding!"

Presently, I resumed our conversation: "It would be a good haul, though, if we could land 'em. You know they wouldn't be smuggling a small amount in a boxcar. It's either liquor or dope. But the chances are we'd have a gunfight about it."

"Yeah. Two tomato cars broke into night before last. One sealed with a U.S. Customs seal. I tell ya, they can't get by with that much longer. It's a thousand-dollar fine to break a Customs seal."

"That's all the more reason, Lawrence, why we've got to make this catch right away. Another month and they won't be operating."

"I don't know about that. That railroad 'bull' says they've been doing it three months now — and nobody's caught 'em yet."

"No, and it's going to be hard to ever get 'em. Working the way they do. They may be dumping that stuff off anywhere between here and Mexico and that's seventy miles of track. How are fifteen men going to watch seventy miles?"

"Damfino, boy, the only way I see it is to hobo it up on the train like we did the other night. And it didn't look like we had any howling success, did it?"

"No. and as I said before, I believe that brakeman knew us. Otherwise, he'd have put us off. Don't you know they won't let bums ride on a train they're smuggling on. He let us ride that night to throw us off the scent. Doesn't seem any use to try *that* anymore; I don't know what we can try. Unless. . .unless. . ." I broke off in silence.

"All right, out with it," Sipe said after a pause. "What'd you start to say?"

"Ah, nothing for now. But there comes our train. It's slipped up on us. We have to hurry!"

We went down the track, Sipe on one side, I on the other. The rumble of the train became louder, but with a slower rhythm. Realizing that it would stop before the usual place, and before we reached it, I broke into a fast run, holding my flashlight in my left hand and my revolver holster firmly against my hip with the other. The road bed of the track was built up of stones, heaped here and there into small piles. Not using the flashlight, running in the darkness, I shortly tripped over one of the heaps. I pitched headlong, catching myself on my hands, and sliding over the rocks. A sharp pain shot into my left hand, and I cursed in an agony of torn flesh and fingernail.

On my feet in a moment, I continued running toward the train.

Then, realizing that the train had stopped nearby, I dropped and lay with head raised, watching the engine and its long string of cars. I knew they were full of perishables from Mexico, tomatoes, peppers, lettuce, coming up from the warm southern lands to be served on the tables of los Yanquís del Norte. In at least one of those cars of tomatoes, in the space left for ventilation between the two loose doors, I thought, there'll be many cases of contraband liquor or narcotics. Else, why did the engineer stop far short of his junction stop?

I watched, but nothing happened. The train stopped only a moment, and then went on. I lowered my head, and the blinding glare of the headlights swept over me and beyond. When the click, click of the car wheels passed, I retraced my steps, flipping off the blood from my hand. Up the track a way I found Lawrence, who had not bothered to run so fast; and we returned to the car. Another night with no positive results! This bothers me more than it does Lawrence, I thought. Perhaps, Navy-trained, I'm bothered too much about my duty. But I probably won't change. I'm just built that way.

We found the railroad 'bull' in the Tucson yards, after his inspection of the train we had watched. "Two seals broken," he said calmly.

"What!" I exclaimed.

"Yep. Two cars, alongside each other. One peppers, the other tomatoes. Looks like they broke into the peppers by mistake. There's dirt tracks in the tomato car where they moved the stuff. It's booze or dope, no doubt about it."

"Well, I don't think they take it off at the junction," Sipe said. "No use meeting the train there any more."

"Right," I agreed. And I resolved to put into action the individualistic plan I had conceived that night.

The next day I went into the office of the Chief Patrol Inspector for Arizona who was then headquartered in Nogales.

The Chief, named Miller, was a tall, well-built man with a very light complexion, not very sunburned for he stayed out of the Arizona sun as much as his job permitted. In this dangerous infancy of the Border Patrol, he liked to employ as inspectors cowmen and military men, both experienced in handling guns.

"Chief," I said, "I have a plan to capture those boxcar smugglers from the source of the contraband. And I'd like your permission to put it into effect."

Miller, listening, did not reply. And I continued, "I find that most of those tomato cars broken into originate at a little Mexican town named Menono in Sonora. What I propose to do is pose as a tramp, A Spaniard, because I talk Castilian Spanish better than the Mexican type, and get a job helping load the boxcars with the tomatoes."

The Chief asked for other details of the plan; and after an hour's conference he approved the mission.

Using the alias Ricardo Martínez, I arrived in Menono unkempt, unshaven, wearing faded, worn overalls, old shoes, and a much-worn peon-style straw hat, and traveling in a tramp's boxcar "side-door pullman." In my duffle bag I had my revolver, concealed in a few clothes.

Menono, including all its component parts, impressed me as a town of dirt. Many of the adobe houses and their surrounding walls seemed to be slowly crumbling into the dirt from whence they came. Some of the houses were enclosed by fences of dead brush of a dirt-brown color and the faces of all those I saw were very brown. I realized I had been correct in not attempting to pass as a Mexican laborer. My fair-white skin would have revealed my lack of the peon's considerable Indian blood.

Seeing a tiendita already open this early in the morning, I entered and accosted its owner, a little Chinese with a multitude of wrinkles in his small, old face.

"How goes it, Juan?" I said in Spanish.

The little man's face lit up in a smile, "Muy bien, Señor, y usted?"

I replied that my health was fine, observed that it was a fine morning, and, laying down two pesos, called for a can of sardines and box of crackers. These I ate, smacking my lips, for I wanted to appear plebian in all things. Then I drank some water from a greasy-looking glass, and was ready to do business. I told "Juan" that I was looking for work, and asked about employment conditions in that town.

"Ah, bueno, bueno! Would the Señor like to pack tomatoes?"

Elated, I replied that in Spain I had been considered a good packer of fruit. Then the Chinese accompanied me to the door, and pointed out a long, low adobe building. Along its side extended a spur of railroad track on which sat numerous box cars.

"Los Señores Pérez, Los Señores Don Juan y Don Hilario, dan trabajo a mucha gente."

By ten o'clock that morning I was at work wrapping tomatoes and placing them in cases. But two days later I was not congratulating myself on good luck, nor did I watch closely enough to see what was going into the boxes of all those working in the room. I'm too vulnerable to a pretty woman, I thought. Nevertheless, I was mainly interested in one pretty, charming face, that of Margarita

Barrón. My glances seemed to disconcert her, for she would look at me and then look elsewhere as she automatically wrapped and packed tomatoes.

Her face was roundish; her skin smooth olive; her hair a glossy brown, her dark-brown eyes were large, and fringed with thin midnight lashes. There were lights and smouldering depths in those eyes, I thought. And the strangely attractive mystery of Mexico! I was fascinated by those sparkling eyes, and fascinated by the mysteriously appealing aura of her dark-eyed youth. But: I must get hold of myself, I thought. I am a happily married man. And I have duty to perform.

At night I slept in the building, with the permission of Don Hilario Pérez, one of the owners. He was in charge of the inside work, including wrapping, packing and the office work, and his brother Juan bossed the men outside.

Hilario was a slender, fine-featured man, with a small, very dark mustache. I had taken an instinctive dislike to him, I knew not why. The next day, however, I was to learn the reason.

"Margarita," I said in Spanish the following morning, as her little hands moved swiftly in wrapping tomatoes, "how do you come to have such polished fingernails? I don't understand it."

She was dressed in white cotton stockings and the cheap, flaming dress of the young Mexican *pelado*.

Fire flashed from her dark eyes and the proud look in her face and erect bearing seemed to intensify.

"And so you think, do you Señor Spaniard, that because a girl is born into a low station of life she cannot always be clean?"

"It just seemed strange."

A flush mantled her cheek; and she turned haughtily to her work.

Then I felt someone's eyes on me, and turned to fully meet the hostile glance of Hilario Pérez.

I looked again at Margarita and saw that her angry look had disappeared. She was smiling at me, and the slumberous look in her dark eyes was intoxicating.

"Forgive me," she said in low, musical Spanish. "Naturally, you regard me as what I am. I am what people call a *peon* or *pelado*; but I keep my nails polished because I don't want to wrap tomatoes all my life." Her voice became a little louder: "I have studied stenography in my spare time; and now I have hopes of going into the office soon."

Again her eyes spoke to mine after the fashion of feminine magic but the next instant she was smiling at Don Hilario. A keen disappointment smote me as I realized she had flirted with me for Hilario's benefit. I seized tomatoes and began wrapping furiously, burning with anger at her and at Hilario.

Day after day I wrapped tomatoes alongside Margarita Barrón; and day after day her strange, proud beauty enchanted me the more.

And night after night I prowled about, watching in vain for smuggled goods to be loaded. At length, I concluded that the loading must be in the daytime.

On the fourth night as I lay on the packed-clay floor half asleep, with the piquant face of Margarita Barrón before me in fantasy, I heard a familiar sound as from far off, the hum of a high-speed internal combustion engine. It sounded like an approaching airplane.

The sound became louder and louder, and I jumped up and ran out of the building. The moon was full, the sky cloudless, and the landscape almost bright as day. The airplane was plainly visible, flying low several hundred yards away. Then I saw it land.

I ran back, put on my shoes and started toward the spot where it had come down. Presently I heard voices; and I hid in the shadow of an old deserted adobe hut. In the neighborhood some of the many dogs were barking.

The voices came nearer and I was startled to recognize the two approaching figures: Hilario and Margarita!

I shrank back into the shadow. They passed not a dozen feet away. Hilario cursed, picked up a stone and flung it at a barking dog. Margarita laughed, low, musical; and the sound set me aflame with helpless anger. They passed on, Margarita holding Hilario's arm.

I returned to my packed-earth bed, lonely, dejected, angry. And I knew I should not feel that way.

The next morning I worked morosely, refusing to speak to anyone. When I looked in Margarita's direction I made it seem as though I were unaware of her presence.

Her look at me was straight and direct, and there was something in her eyes that seemed to indicate sadness. I thought she had come to realize the wide, nearly impassable gulf between our two ways of life. Some instinct in her being apparently had warned her that she was not for me. Yet, such is the alchemy of power of romantic love: Regardless of my marriage, I thought, I love her. I can't help it. Man is basically polygamous by nature. I'm just built that way. Yet I do love my wife.

Margarita laid a small hand on my arm. With a touch that sent an electric shock through me.

"What is the matter, my friend? Don't you feel well this morning?"

"No, Margarita. I'm young. But I guess at the moment I am really tired of life. I think I'll leave here soon."

"Oh, no," she said. "Not for a while yet, Ricardo. Just for a little while yet!"

Then a moment later she spoke low: "Listen, Ricardo. If they try to put you outside loading the cars, don't you do it. It isn't good. There are things they do that are not good. No good for you!"

"What are they doing?" I asked. But she shut up like a clam.

Presently, Hilario came and walked toward me. He spoke abruptly: "Martínez, my brother Juan says that when he hired you, you said you'd like to work outside."

"I did," I replied, leaving off the customary "Señor." I was a poor detective. Not very able to conceal my feelings.

"Well, then, you may go out there now, and begin work if you still wish to."

I hesitated, uncertain. If I left this room, my association with Margarita would end. No longer would I be intoxicated by her nearness. Of course, that is what I ought to do. If I went outside I'd have at least a better chance of succeeding in my mission.

I looked at Margarita, and her eyes were pleading. They seemed to say, "Stay! Stay!"

I am sorry to say, my infatuation won over reason and duty. "No. I have changed my mind. I don't want to work outside."

Hilario cursed, spun on his heel, and left with angry steps.

"I dislike him," Margarita said.

"So do I."

In an hour or so Hilario returned and walking up to Margarita said something in a low voice, and patted her on the shoulder. Holding a hard green tomato in my hand, I stared at them. I saw Margarita shrink slightly from the man's touch. Then he slipped his arm around her shoulder; and I saw red. I threw the tomato with all the force of a former baseball player and hit my rival on the head. With a frightful oath he turned and charged.

I hit him hard with clenched fist. And he went down.

The place was in an uproar. Just as Juan, the older brother, came in, Hilario rose with blood in his eye.

57

"You're fired," he roared, threateningly advancing toward me.

Juan laid his hand on his brother, "He is *not* fired. You'll fire no more men that *I* hire, Hilario. *I* am boss here. If you attended to your work more instead of hanging around this girl, you wouldn't have so much trouble."

He made a gesture for me to accompany him and together we left the room. I had clearly demonstrated that I was no detective but I was not sorry. I had seen Margarita shrink from the touch of that dog, Hilario, and I was glad that I had hit him.

That afternoon, as I labored outside, loading the cars, my spirits were lowered by the news that Margarita had been taken into the office as Hilario's stenographer.

The next day, just before quitting time, I discovered what I had been looking for. A car half-loaded with tomatoes was being completed with liquor. In the morning it would be sealed and sent away.

I was both excited and saddened. My duty compelled me to carry out the original plan; to get my duffel bag, buy a little food from the Chinese man's store and conceal myself in the car and ride with it until it was opened for removal of the liquor. Then I would make the arrests, including the train employees. The Customs officer who failed to inspect the car would also be apprehended and in time perhaps many of the smuggling syndicate. But I was saddened because if I left in this manner Margarita Barrón would drop out of my life. Can I leave her now? I thought gloomily. I can wait only a little while!

My day's work ended, and I entered the long, low business building, still undecided. Then I heard voices in the office. I drew near and listened.

"Why go tomorrow?" I heard Margarita say. "I can go just as well day after tomorrow and get there in plenty of time. This American Chief that you call Beeg Boy won't arrive at the border for three days yet, that is if he left New York as he planned."

"Why don't you want to go?" snarled Hilario. "Is it that vagabond lover of yours? Maybe I'll kill him, my fine Señorita. It may interest you to know that he has become part of our smuggling machine. I'll send him to the States soon, and tip off the officers there and then that'll be the end of your tramp sweetheart."

Peeping in through a crack in the door that stood ajar, I saw Margarita standing there, her face flushed with anger. Then Hilario grabbed her and forcibly drew her to him. She screamed. I flung open the door and charged. I seized the man by the throat, and with my knee in his stomach began slowly to choke him to death.

I heard Margarita scream, "Ricardo! Behind you!" Releasing Hilario and whirling, I saw Juan coming toward me from the other room, a dagger in his hand.

Things happened swiftly. Just as Juan, dagger aimed, was springing at me, Margarita produced from somewhere a tiny revolver and fired. Juan fell dead at my feet.

"Come!" she cried. "We must hurry!"

When we emerged, people were coming from every direction.

"There are the police!" cried Margarita. "Juan owns them."

We ran furiously. Margarita suddenly turned into a wide building, and without knowing why I followed.

A Mexican youth jumped to his feet.

"The airplane!" she ordered. "Come out and start it!"

Then she seized two helmets, and turning led the way to a plane that stood outside. Handing me one of the helmets, she took the other and crawled into the front seat of the cockpit. Wondering, I went in behind her.

The youth spun the propeller at her command. It did not start.

I heard shouts from behind.

Again the boy spun the propeller, and this time the engine exploded with a roar.

I looked back. A crowd was running toward us. Two men in the lead began to shoot.

The engine roared and we were off at a fast speed down the level field. Then with a rush, the airplane rose, circled and to my surprise, headed northward toward the United States.

Of course, there was no canopy on the fuselage; and when I stuck my head up, the wind seemed about to blow it off. In the noise, no conversation was possible. I settled back and was considering the strange turn of events. What am I to think about all this? One thing seems sure; she's one of the gang! No pelado at all, but a flier who works with them. I'll have to give her name as one of the smugglers and I'll need even to arrest her if I see her land in the United States. But would I want to? Could I do that? When I love her, and she has saved my life.

I saw that the plane was still headed north, toward the United States. Well, it's an awful mess I've got into. It's hell to be young and so romantic as I am. I, Patrol Inspector Richard Morton, married to a good wife, love a female Mexican smuggler! Faced with the necessity of arresting her, if she lands on the U.S. side. Of course, I could just let her go. But could I, long steeped in the concept of adherence to duty, do that?

If she landed in the U.S., I saw no way, being myself, but to arrest her for smuggling. Unlike little Victoria, I thought, she is a bad criminal. She is no *pelado* worker at all, but a flier and an important one of the smuggling gang.

The lights of a town, coming on near dusk, came into view. I recognized Nogales, Sonora and then Nogales, Arizona!

We landed, the engine's roar ceased, and somewhat stiff from cold, I crawled out.

We stopped in the shadow of an unlighted hanger.

"Margarita," I said softly.

"Wait, Ricardo!" she said, and her voice trembled. "I have a duty that is greater than my love for you. Ricardo, my Ricardo—I—" she faltered, and took her little revolver from her purse. "I am not a Mexican *pelado*. I am a Mexican-American," and she added proudly, "of a good family of Mexico and Spain. I am an officer of the U.S. Government, the Customs Service. I'm sorry, Ricardo, but I *must* arrest you, and hold you as a material witness to smuggling."

I was too stunned to reply. She must have taken my silence for reproach.

"*Diós mío!*" she cried. "I *cannot* do it. I can't hold you *even* as just a witness." She put the gun back in her purse. "Go, Ricardo, go! May the blessing of *Diós* go with you!"

"Not Ricardo! Richard!" I exclaimed. "Richard Morton of the Border Patrol. Why don't you talk in your own language, my dear Margarita!"

"Well, what do you know about that!" she exclaimed in English, and fell into my arms. I could not immediately tell her I was married but a little later I leveled with her. "Margarita," I said, "apparently both of our missions have failed. Because of our love. But, que será, será."

"*Sí,*" she smiled. "But don't worry, my dear Richard. In the office I found the names of the brakemen involved. We can find out what trains they're on. And then some Spanish *tramp* who can ride freight trains, maybe you, Ricardo, can arrest them. Also the Customs Inspector, the traitor, who is approving entry of those cars. And we both can serve as witnesses against Hilario."

"Yeah. If we can catch him on this side of the line."

"Oh, we will. Every Mexican with money comes to *la tierra de los Yanquis.*"

And that is how I, and later also my wife, became long-time friends with Margarita Barrón, secret officer and Inspector of the United States Customs Service.

CHAPTER 6
At the Pass

What happened in the Baboquivari Mountains on that August night of 1927 seems unbelievable but it was an unforgettable experience.

When the Chief Patrol Inspector summoned three of us into his office, we wondered what was to be our next assignment. For our life as Patrol Inspectors of the new U.S. Border Patrol between the still somewhat primitive new state of Arizona and turbulent but fascinating Old Mexico was quite uncertain. We never knew when we'd need to "shoot it out" with smugglers of aliens, liquor or narcotics.

We three were very unlike. But all came within the willing-to-fight category that the Chief and the U.S. Civil Service seemed to prefer as "watchdogs" on the dangerous Mexican Border: Charley Myers, cockily short, formerly of the Nogales Police Force at the Border; ex heavyweight prizefighter Herbert Stoner, a blond giant of a man with a plate in his broken jaw that made him quit the boxing ring, mostly hard of countenance, but sometimes magnetically, almost boyishly, pleasant; and myself. We had three things in common: British-descent, Spanish-speaking, although Stoner's was rather sketchy; and all of us were skilled in shooting.

As was his wont, the Chief looked hard at us. Yet when he spoke his voice was soft, almost a Texas drawl: "You three are among my best officers. So I'm assigning you to a dangerous job."

A good executive, I thought. Compliments us before he sends us out, maybe to die.

"As you know," he continued, "we recently lost two good men, killed by those damned smuggling aliens. At the line west of Sasabe in the Baboquivari Mountains. I have received a tip that in the next few days they're planning to come in, hot and heavy. One is a murderer we have failed to catch. Twice he has murdered and escaped from prison. He'll waylay you and try to kill you from behind. I believe there's no arresting that man alive. Try but don't give him a chance to kill you."

"Stoner, I'm putting you in charge. Charley, I realize you know the country there, but —" and here he looked hard at Stoner, "maybe more responsibility, Herb, will make you treat aliens better. Oh, I know a lot of things you've done, like tying that Mexican smuggler behind your horse and forcing him to run behind you or be dragged through the rocks and cacti."

Herb interposed: "I got the truth out of him."

"Yes, I know, but that's not the way to do it. You've got to improve. If you don't, and I get one more report of your mistreatment of aliens, I'll have to wade through red tape to fire you." He smiled. "If some Mexican woman's husband or boyfriend doesn't kill you first!"

"Take the station wagon, men. Carry enough food to last a week. Camp at the pass. Take enough blankets. It's very cold at night there. Nearby Baboquivari peak is nearly eight thousand feet high. And Herb, I warn you, your boxing fists are lethal weapons, according to law. Don't hit any aliens! That's all. Any questions?"

There were none. So he said, "Good luck! You may need it."

As we rose to leave, the Chief asked me to stay behind a moment. After the other two were gone, he said, "Morton, I'm going to rely on you and Charley to try to keep Stoner from brutal treatment of aliens. In a way, he's afraid of nothing and a dead shot. In these hot prohibition and drug-smuggling times, I don't want to lose him."

"Aye, aye, sir," I responded, using the old Navy term. "I'll do the best I can. Herb's like a wild stallion."

We headed out, loaded with our usual camping goods: our bedrolls and food, mostly beans, salt pork to put in the beans, canned vegetables, cabbage and prunes.

A strange thing about Herbert Stoner was his strong attraction for women, especially Mexican women. Sometimes he had been severely reprimanded about his affairs with alien girls some of whom actually had been debarred from the U.S., but somehow had managed to get through or around the Garita from Mexico, subsequently later to be found by the Border Patrol.

One attraction about Herb Stoner was his devil-may-care way. A lot of us, men and women, are rebels at heart; and although we cautiously don't flaunt our dislike of the Establishment we have a certain admiration for one who does. Herbert Stoner seemed to do just whatever he wanted to do and to hell with the consequences!

We drove a few miles and then Stoner spotted some geese in a ditch. It had been raining, the kind of weather waterfowl loved. Herb stopped the car, and took out the axe we always carried on camping trips.

Charley and I objected to what we knew he was going to do: "They're private property, Stoner." But he flung back at us, "Necessity knows no law! We need fresh meat."

And he began running the geese down. Well, he killed one of them with the axe, brought it back to the car, and then silently drove on.

At our destination we camped two uneventful nights. And then on the third what we were there for happened. A smuggler came on foot, carrying a heavy load in a sack. We drew our guns, and put our car lights on him. He dropped his burden, threw up his hands. I was surprised by his size. He was short, not even as tall as Charley, and smooth-faced and young.

"Search him, Morton," Stoner said. When I frisked him, I had a shock of great surprise! There were no weapons in his pockets. Unlike most men I had searched, his hips were rather large. In my search I came to his chest; and then a fact dawned on me. The "he" was no he at all. He was obviously a woman for when my hand passed over her breast the feminine softness there was quite round and attractive.

Almost as in a daze, I automatically passed my hand over her legs and into the capacious boots that she wore, probably a man's boots.

"No weapons on him," I said. Wisely, I thought, I used the terms "him." She would safe with Charley as she was with me. But Stoner?!

Charley began questioning "him" in his native-type Spanish patois. I joined and Herb occasionally came in with his poor Spanish for he knew very little about the language.

The woman kept insisting that she had found the smuggled liquor and narcotics under a bush this side of the line. Occasionally, Stoner angrily turned to English, which the smuggler obviously did not understand. I could tell Herb's patience for the woman's flimsy story was about to run out. Suddenly he strode to the car, and returned with a rope. Then he towered above the poor woman, making a noose in the line. "Vé este," he angrily asked. "If you don't tell us the truth, I'm going to hang you!"

I felt very sorry for the trembling, badly frightened girl. Then she startled me, for she broke into a mad dash for freedom, going not down the road but off to our left down the side of a canyon. I snatched my gun and was about to fire into the air, when a rifle flash shot past my side. Charley, who had kept his Winchester in hand, had fired it down the canyon.

The poor woman abruptly stopped her flight, panting in terror and exertion.

Stoner fiercely grabbed her in his huge arms. Then he must have felt the same softness I had, for obviously the truth dawned on him: that we had a *woman* smuggler as prisoner.

When he began jerking open her jacket to see for himself her nudity, I knew the fat was in the fire. He would have her half stripped and prone in the station wagon in short order.

Quickly, I wondered what to do. I decided that Charley with his rigid brother-officer code would do nothing. I knew that if Stoner began to rape her I'd pull my gun on him.

Things were happening too quickly. The girl suddenly reached into one of those oversize boots where, apparently deep down, she had a scabbard and knife. She snatched it out, and in an instant stabbed Stoner with all her strength. She struck to the heart. He fell.

Charley grabbed the woman, forced the knife out of her hand, and I knelt beside Stoner. Blood was pouring from his wounded heart and I knew there was no hope for poor Herb. He lay there a little while dying, then went out of this life as he had lived, unafraid.

In a way I had liked this devil-may-care comrade-at-arms. And briefly, I grieved for him. I grieved also for that pretty smuggler. Only God and a jury would know what would happen to her. The smuggling of liquor and dope was bad enough, but now she also had a charge of murder against her.

Momentarily, I grieved for her and for a mixed-up former heavyweight fighter who had never grown up. Then Charley and I picked up the dead body of our fellow officer, put it and our gear in the car and set out for Headquarters. Charley drove and I was in back with the frightened woman.

I tried to ease her worried mind a bit. I told her I'd testify as to the facts and that would help her some with the jury. But I knew that she'd be lucky to escape life imprisonment for killing a U.S. officer. "No Tenga miedo," I said. "Do not be afraid."

It was a long time before I could erase the sadness I felt about our Baboquivari Mountains adventure. I knew that once again I had done my duty as a member of the U.S. Border Patrol and yet — yet I felt that Herb Stoner had been responsible for the tragic turn of events and thus the arrest of the poor woman whose original crime would have been comparatively minor. If it had not been for that unfortunate meeting she would be back in Mexico and Herb would still be alive.

CHAPTER 7
Hard Luck Canyon

We of the Border Patrol were on duty long hours and nearly every day but we did take some time for recreation: target practice; occasional motion pictures; rodeos; barbecues (of whole beeves); and hunting. For most of us hunting was our preferred pastime.

I prefer hunting quail but I have hunted deer, and once in a great adventure, involving a fateful ravine, Hard Luck Canyon. I was hunting with a new friend, Immigration Inspector Joe Gates, a former "hard-rock miner" who, like me, loved the outdoors and the wild country.

In this hunt we were resting on a side hill, facing a long, wide canyon, with a mountain to its left. Joe, myself and "Old Man Simpson," a widower, who had volunteered to be our guide. I think he liked to hunt with others partly to dispel his loneliness.

"See that long bench, there where the line of rock is, about three-fourths up?" Old Man Simpson asked.

Then, without waiting for a reply, he drawled on, "There's where we'll find our deer. This time of the year the old bucks love to hide around the base of them crags, where it's wild and not many people come."

"But for God's sake, boys —" he took his corncob pipe from his mouth and regarded us two young men, his wrinkled blue eyes serious, his twisted nose shining red, "Whatever you do, don't go into that canyon on the right end — there where the bench breaks." He pointed a skinny old finger.

"Why?" Joe asked.

"That's Hard Luck Canyon," he said, lowering his voice. "Boys, it's a fact that in the last fourteen deer seasons, to my knowledge nine hunters have been shot up in that canyon." He paused.

"Shot? How do you mean?" I asked.

"That's the question," he said. "Nobody knows. It may be they was shot by other hunters that took 'em for deer, I don't know. Bill Kane, the last one, was killed four years ago today. Bill Kane had killed his own shootin' partner the year before, thinkin' he was a deer, so it might have been poetical justice in his case. I don't know. I remember well the first one what was shot. I'd just come to this country then, had a prospect up Three-R Canyon."

He coaxed his pipe back to life.

"I knowed this boy's dad by sight. A long, slim mountaineer from Tennessee by the name of Jim Thornton. I remember he had a funny-shaped scar on his forehead, shaped a little like a cross. The funniest thing you ever saw. The Mexicans all called him "El Hombre de la Santa Cruz." The man of the Holy Cross, you know. When he got mad that cross was red as fire. He was a crazy sort of fellow, always kept to hisself, him and his son Abe. Jim's wife had died and he raised Abe up by hisself. That boy was the only interest he had in life."

Old Man Simpson took his pipe from his mouth, spat expertly into a maguey plant, gazed for a moment at a buzzard in the hard, brilliant bowl that was the sky, and then continued, "Well, the day deer season opened, fourteen years ago today, the boy went out huntin' alone and like a lot of others he never come back. A searchin' party found him lyin' in that canyon over there — shot dead. Don't ask me how. I don't know. Another hunter mighta shot him for a deer, and then got scared and went on home without sayin' nothin' about it. And maybe not.

"Jim Thornton didn't say much, didn't shed a tear, but his eyes, I'm tellin' you, wasn't good to look at. Two days later they took him to the insane asylum, stark mad. So that's the reason, boys, I'm tellin' ya, don't go near that canyon. It's hard luck. God knows how many hunters died there before Abe Thornton got his, but since then to my knowledge eight men has been shot. As I say, I don't know how. You can't never prove nothin', just a bullet hole through the body, that's all. The Indians say it ain't no *earthly* bullet."

I said, "This reminds me of some awfully mysterious facts written about by a strange writer. Have you ever heard of Charles Fort?"

Neither had. So I continued, "He got interested in mysteries which have been published and then promptly forgotten. He's published two books, *The Book of the Damned* and *New Lands*; and I understand is working on another.

"Anyway, among a great many other mysteries, he's written

about unexplained shots, almost as by a ghost. But I believe those things have some logical explanation, if we could just find it. For instance, *Popular Science* had an account about a man in Germany who was pushing a cart when something like a bullet went through his right arm, and left no sign but a hole. All he had heard was a whir. Nobody was within gunshot distance of him. And an oil cask, strangely, was holed by many mysterious things that apparently just disappeared. And windows in Newark, New Jersey were mysteriously perforated. What do you think of that?"

Old Man Simpson did not answer. I had the feeling he thought I was "talking through my hat." But Joe, I knew, was somewhat interested in strange events, although he preferred humorous stories. But now he said, "Richard, I take all such stories with a grain of salt. Maybe some are true, but I prefer not to be bothered by them."

His reply didn't surprise me. I knew there would be no use to mention many other strange items in the press found and written about by Charles Fort. For instance, a space island above us that ordinarily was invisible but showed up in a picture. And strange forces from the sky that have lifted a large number of objects into the air, some far into the sky where they disappeared and even a heavy fishing boat lifted so far that when it fell back it sank. And people who suddenly have been taken off the earth, never to be seen again.

But these subjects hardly seemed appropriate in a deer hunt. Except, perhaps, because of the possibility of "unearthly" bullets in Hard Luck Canyon. Not probably, I thought. So I put the whole matter out of my mind, and turned to the atavistic pleasure of the hunt.

I looked again to where the invisible Hard Luck Canyon dropped from the break in the long rocky ledge. The intervening mountain slope did not smile with green, as some hills do. It was a tawny, silent monster, lying with fangs bared beneath the pitiless sun. The depressing silence of the desert momentarily weighed upon me. This was a hard land, somber, merciless, charged with something that hinted of the grave and yet, I had come to love it.

"Well, let's get started," said Joe. "Maybe we'll have good luck near this Hard Luck Canyon."

We rose and followed a deer trail down the steep hillside.

"Look here, boys," said Old Man Simpson.

He pointed at a place where the brown grass had been crushed in a small circle. "Here's where a deer slept last night and there's another." He pointed a little farther down the hill.

"They're here, all right," said Joe, in an encouraged tone.

"Yes, they're here," said Old Man Simpson. "It's the light of the moon now, you see, and they come out here to feed at night. When they're full, they lie down and rest a while."

"Look here, Joe," I said excited a little. "Here are their fresh leavings. We'll get one before sundown."

"I'll say we will," Joe heartily agreed.

A few minutes later he pointed out a place where quail had bedded. A few feathers lay about the spot. "All kinds of signs," he said. "Where's the game?"

Farther down, there was a sudden drum of wings and a covey of quail shot from under Old Man Simpson's feet. "There's part of your game," he said. "I wish they was in season."

"I sure hope we find the other part," I replied and hurried on like a dog on warm scent.

At the bottom, Old Man Simpson turned down the canyon, and Joe and I toiled up the opposite side, following a faint deer trail.

"Old Man Simpson's pretty wise, isn't he?" remarked Joe. "Taking the lower course and using us as gamebeaters to run the deer down to him. Pretty wise."

"You know, I thought of that myself. But he's getting old, he's been there before. Maybe you and I will be wise like that when we get old."

We came to the first fold in the slope and I turned to the right through the stunted trees, while Joe continued to ascend toward the line of rocky crags.

No sooner was Joe out of sight than I slowed down, to give him time to reach the top. Thus, we both would start around the mountain at the same time and any deer Joe jumped would run down by me and I would get a shot before Old Man Simpson, and vice versa. Every man for himself, including the deer, I thought.

I held my rifle in readiness and moved over the slope as silently as possible. At every rise of ground and the top of every canyon I moved very cautiously, watching for the slightest movement, listening for the smallest sound.

Disappointed as I crossed each canyon, I always hoped again at sight of the next. There was a great deal of fresh deer signs. Well-worn trails intersected my course, many of the tracks still moist. But the deer always had moved on into the next canyon.

In this way, oblivious to time, distance and everything except the hunt, I must have covered some two miles, when all at once I realized that I had reached the end of my allotted course and must turn down the wide canyon at my feet. For, just beyond, lay Hard Luck Canyon. A little chill of apprehension ran up and down my spine, as I recalled Old Man Simpson's gruesome tale. Old Man Simpson, like most "hard-rock" miners, I thought, is not inclined toward being superstitious.

I quickened my steps to descend, when suddenly there was a crackling noise, like some large animal going through the brush ahead. I stopped still, heart pounding, eyes penetrating as well as possible through the stunted mesquite, my rifle ready. The sound had also stopped. I moved to the right and the noise broke out again. Surely it was some mighty buck moving down the wall of the canyon.

In a minute the animal reached the floor of the ravine and began running up the opposite slope toward Hard Luck Canyon. Then I saw what it was, a large buck of about fourteen points. Quickly I threw my rifle to shoulder and fired.

An involuntary curse escaped my lips, realizing I had missed. The buck's white tail bobbed up and down over the boulders, making him a difficult target. I aimed carefully, just over his head, and shot again.

The deer stumbled and fell. A wild primordial joy surged through my heart, only to break into intense disappointment a moment later as the animal rose, stumbled over the crest and disappeared toward the ill-fated canyon.

"Joe!" I yelled at the top of my voice. "Joe!"

The barren crags took up my voice and flung it back, weirdly changed. "Simpson!" I shouted. "Simpson!" Profound silence.

For a moment I hesitated, torn between fear of the unknown and the hot desire of the chase. Then the hunting instinct conquered and I tore through the brush and over boulders in the direction the deer had gone.

I came to a crimson trail that led over the rim and hurried on to the very edge of Hard Luck Canyon.

Its appearance was worthy of its name, barren, steep-walled, with a narrow, rocky gorge at the base. To my right, there was a precipitous break in the gorge, where rapids fell during the rainy season. Just now the boulder-strewn course looked empty, purposeless, a place where water had died.

I hesitated a moment, in the clutch of a nameless fear, then set my jaw and plunged down the steep slope.

The next few minutes, eyes glued to the ground, I struggled to keep my footing on the rocky way. Then my feet slid from under me amid noise of falling stones and my right wrist struck the sharp-edged sword of a maguey plant. I rose and cautiously continued to descend.

Near the gorge at the bottom I paused a moment and studied the surrounding terrain. Then my heart leaped, as I saw the wonderful buck, lying dead a short distance down the canyon. I started toward it.

Suddenly the sharp crack of a rifle came. I stopped. Fear seized me, and then I chided myself for a supersititous one. Joe had fired at a deer somewhere. Perhaps at me, thinking I was a deer. Of course!

"Joe!" I shouted, "Oh, Joe!" Again the crags made a weird mockery of my voice.

I opened my mouth to shout again and then realized that probably Joe was too far away to hear.

Suddenly, from out of the cloudless sky, the report came again. And this time I distinctly heard the whine of a bullet.

I lay still, just as I had fallen, breathing heavily, my heart pounding. Then my brain got busy. I couldn't lie there forever, I reasoned. Who could the unknown assailant be? Some nervous hunter, perhaps, who had mistaken me for a deer? Of course, that was all.

I turned my head and shouted: "Hey! Don't shoot down here! Don't shoot! There's no deer here."

Not a sound broke the autumnal silence. It was not Joe, I told myself, for Joe would have heard and answered. Who was it then? Was it anybody? My mouth and throat were dry. Could it be that my imagination was playing tricks? Could both shots have been the product of my mind?

Still lying down, I cautiously removed my hunting coat and then held it up on a stick. Again the rifle cracked and I saw a small, round hole that had appeared in the coat. That hole was something material. One who strangely was my enemy was firing on me with the clear intent of murder. Old Man Simpson had been right. Hard Luck Canyon! I thought of the nine men who had been killed in this ill-starred spot.

To my right a small ravine meandered toward the narrow gorge. I noted that its course was approximately perpendicular to the line of fire from the unseen gun.

Suddenly I leaped to my feet and dashed pell-mell into it, scattering rocks downhill. Two shots sounded and a sharp pain stabbed my left shoulder. Safely under cover, I investigated the hurt, and was pleased to note that it was only a flesh wound. The sight of my blood made me deadly calm.

I made my way down the little ravine toward an oak tree. Just before reaching it, I laid my hat on the bank above, in view of the opposite slope. Then slowly I rose behind the tree and peeped around its trunk.

I studied the opposite slope and could not discern a sign of life. But presently a report sounded again and my hat was knocked into the ravine. Then I saw the assailant, behind a large boulder, about half way up on the other side. The long barrel of his gun was resting by the side of the boulder.

Quickly I raised my rifle, took aim and fired. Apparently I missed. The man's sharp eyes saw me and the next instant a bullet whined by my ear.

I aimed again and very carefully aligned my sights. Cool! I never was so calm. My life depended, perhaps, on that shot. I fired.

The man pitched forward. Then stumbling to his feet, he scrambled up the slope, apparently making for the black mouth of a small cave. Just as he reached its entrance I fired again. He fell and lay still.

This time, I thought grimly, the damned murderer was shooting at the wrong man!

"Joe! Oh, Joe!" I shouted. And then I saw my hunting companion descending toward my ravine.

Leaping out of the gully, I shouted for help. He hurried to my side, scattering stones in his precipitous descent.

"What's the matter, Richard? Why were you shooting?"

I sketched in a few words the strange things that had happened. Then we climbed the opposite hill.

Did you ever find a bird you had shot dead with its head in a hole? That was the way I felt when I saw that crumpled figure lying at my feet, so near to the cave.

Joe turned over the body. It was a tall, slim man, with hair like a wild man's.

"Hey!" exclaimed Joe. "Look at that!"

The hair stiffened on the back of my neck. Near the hairline of the dead man's forehead was a scar, a large scar in the form of a rough cross!

Joe picked up the man's rifle, a rusty old Winchester. He studied the scarred stock.

"Eight notches," he said. "He must have killed those eight hunters out of revenge for his son." He looked at the upturned face. "How do you suppose he got out of the insane asylum? Do you suppose he was actually crazy?"

The sightless eyes seemed to accuse me. I looked away.

"God knows," I answered. "No more so, perhaps, than the man who shot his son for a deer."

CHAPTER 8
The Good Old Days

On a scouting trip northward of Nogales I met an old trapper. He was certainly no hermit for he had a Mexican-American wife, and despite his advancing years had managed to sire three children. His name was Sank Ritter, "Old Sank" the trapper, he was usually called by those who knew him.

His home was on a rough wagon trail and his means of transportation a cart, drawn by a burro. Life to Old Sank was greatly simplified: three squares a day with meat he killed and in summer and fall vegetables from their garden by the river, mostly worked by his dark-eyed youngish wife, who withdrew when I visited Sank.

Quite unintentionally, he was a humorous individual, for he told tales of his far-ranging travels, much of which obviously was fictional. I doubt that he had ever been out of Arizona. His tales probably had been influenced by what he had heard about the late far-traveled old trapper Tarn, numerous miles north of his adobe hut.

With his old shotgun he once hunted quail with me and white-winged doves. Old Sank knew well where to find them. I gathered that he knew also where to find deer. And after the deer season opened, I went to his place with a new friend by the name of Smith. In the United States there is often nearby a person named Smith, you know, usually called "Smitty." This "Smitty" was a teacher of science in Nogales High School. He came with a double-barreled shotgun. I hoped he would be a good alert marksman and not shoot my way. He had *talked* a good job of shooting. Well, he should for he was born and reared in the mountains of Arizona.

After I introduced him briefly to Old Sank, we sat and talked a while before beginning the deer hunt.

Sank lifted the lid of the combined cooking and heating stove, spat out his chew, nearly big enough to put out the fire. Walking over to the single window of the room, he picked up his old corncob pipe and filled it with some of his poor-quality tobacco.

"Wal, boys," he said in an optimistic tone after he had lifted up and resumed his seat. "We're gonna have luck today. The animals is runnin' fine in these here mountains this year. I already caught six fox, three coyote, two 'coon and a skunk. And the fur's fine. I showed you thet fur, didn't I, Morton? Yes-s-s." He puffed his pipe meditatively.

"Sure," I said. "Good fur for this early in winter."

"Yes-s-s, a lot of animals runnin'. Thet's a good sign. I notice when they's plenty of fur-bearin' animals they's always plenty of deer. I saw lots of tracks up Quail Canyon yesterday. Oh, I'll git both of you a deer, all right. I know deer bettern'n they know theirselves. Yes-s-s."

Sitting with my long legs stretched out in the corner behind the stove, I glanced at Smitty who was a small man, much given to sarcasm. He was now looking at the old trapper with a half-amused, half-cynical smile.

"You mean you'll show us the deer," I said. "And then it'll be up to us and the buck ague."

"Boy, I passed the buck ague stage not long after the cradle," said Smitty. "I was born with a rifle in my hand."

Old Sank looked at him as though he didn't believe it.

"Yeah?" he said. "Wal, I wasn't borned with no rifle in my hand, but I shore have shot 'em in my day. I've killed every kind of animal they is, from lions to a cottontail rabbit."

"What kind of lions — mountain lions, you mean?" I asked.

"No. Genuwine African lions. And elephants the size of a barn. I think I told you, Morton, didn't I, thet I was down to Africa oncet. When I was young I was a wanderer over the face of th' earth. I was in every continent an' I stayed in th' African jungle a while. Yeah. Thet was a long time ago, when th' lions was fierce. I shot many a one from my back door."

"From your back door, man!" expostulated Smitty. "You don't meant it."

"Why sartainly, I mean it. I don't tell lies, you know. Some of them animals was awfully savage. Yes-s-s."

The old man coaxed his pipe back to life and looked at Smith.

"Have you ever been to Africa, Mr. Smith?"

"Sure, I've been to Africa. I've been to Tangiers, across the

Mediterranean from the Rock. There are lots of bears in Tangiers."

"No? Thet's funny. I never heard of no bears in Tangiers."

"Why, of course, there are bears. Pink bears, and pink mice. And that's all those sheiks do, just hunt 'em. They even find them in their harems."

Old Sank stared, as though puzzled.

"Don't pay any attention to Smitty," I said. "He has those spells. But I'm really interested in your experiences, Sank. tell us, what was the closest corner you ever were in — where four-legged animals are concerned?"

The old man puffed meditatively for some time, and then spoke.

"Wal, it was way back — in the good old days when this country was raw, and game was as plentiful as cactus is now. I was prospectin' up in th' Rockies and I had a partner, an Injun he was, by the name of Bitin' Ear.

"An early winter come an' th' snow begin to fly, an' th' animals all trekked. Old Bitin' Ear an' me was on trail of a good minin' prospect whut we didn't want to leave. But meat got scarcer 'n scarcer, an' finely we couldn't stand it no longer, so we headed south. Cold! Boys, you don't know whut cold weather is. Snow twenty feet deep an' th' blizzard bitin' yore face like a wile cat. We don't have cold weather like thet no more. No-o-o.

"Wal, th' game got scarcer 'n scarcer, and finely it got so we was starvin'.

"One day when my belly was techin' my backbone, I was thet hungry, in come Bitin' Ear, an' I could see he was excited, for an Injun. But he didn't say a word — jes' went to our burro an' hauled out two deer skins of his'n. He handed me one an' took the' other.

"'Heap big elk,' he says. 'There!' He points to th' west. We made tracks away from there.

"When we come in sight, I see th' elk was a whopper, ten points, a-grazin' on a patch o' grass thet he pawed th' snow from.

"Bitin' Ear wet his finger an' held it up. Th' wind was in our favor, away from the elk.

"Then we put on deer skins; we wasn't takin' no chances, you see.

"Gentlemen, have you ever walked in a deer skin? Th' danged thing's always slippin', an' walkin' on yore all-fours with a rifle in yore hand ain't so easy, 'specially for a starvin' man. I was tremblin' all over when we got up to safe shootin' distance.

"Then Bitin' Ear went an' played th' dickens. He knowed I was a better shot than him. In them days I was th' best shot in th' whole West. Yes, sir, barrin' none. Don't you believe it? It's a fack. I never missed a deer in my life whut I drawed a bead on.

"But Bitin' Ear, he gits nervous, an' before I could say Jack Robinson, he lets fly.

"The elk turns an' bellows. I see a red spot formin' on his side, but it's too fur back for th' heart.

"I throwed up my gun an' pulled th' trigger. An' whut you know? Th' danged thing snapped on me. An' by thet time th' elk had seed our smoke, an' hyar he come.

"Thar we was, defenseless in them danged deer skins. Anyhow, I thought so until I looks around. Bitin' Ear jes' wasn't thar. He jes' disappeared, hide an' hair. He come from a fast travelin' race an' he shore wasn't no slow poke. Whur he went I don't know. I never seed him again.

"An' anyhow, I wasn't worryin' none about him. It was root hog or die, with thet elk comin' to call. He was some incensed at thet unfriendly bullet of Bitin' Ear's. I took one look at him an' I see murder in his eye. Th' next minute I was chargin' south runnin' on my two laigs in thet deer skin an' I was movin' like a bee. Thorns an' brush wasn't no obstacle to me.

"Thet elk was gainin' an', gentlemen, I jes' knowed I was done for. Them horns was th' biggest I ever seed, an' th' next minute I'd be on 'em.

"I looked for a tree but there wasn't nary a one in sight. Then I spies a hole in the rock cliff nearby.

"In I scooted, deer skin an' all. An' I tell you, gentlemen, I could feel thet elk's hot breath on th' seat of my pants. His horns was so big they jammed at th' entrance, an' kept him from comin' on in. Them was th' biggest horns I ever seed.

"My heart was in my mouth. He was shore mad. He paws an' bellows for a minute, an' then walks back a little. I got holt of my lost breath an' looked around my cave. Then was when I got th' shock of my life.

"I found out I was trespassin'. Th' owner of th' hole was standin' on his hind laigs an' lookin' at me, jes' exactly like them sassiety women look through them glasses at a unwelcome guest. Gentlemen, it was a bear! An' th' biggest bear I ever seed.

"I didn't argue with him none, but jes' th' same he oughta had thet cave of his'n posted. Twarnt' fair atall.

"I didn't reason none about it then, but I reck'n he didn't hug me by way of sayin' hello because he was some surprised at my git-up. He couldn't savvy a deer on two laigs.

"Anyhow, I see by his manner I wasn't welcome, so I backs out, hopin' th' elk was gone.

"But he wasn't. Jes' as soon as I pops out of th' hole, he makes a beeline for me. I war sartainly between th' devil an' th' deep blue sea. I looked around like a drownin' man. There wasn't nary another hole.

"Jes' as th' elk's horns teched th' seat of my pants, I pops back into th' bear's house.

"'Whut? You hyar again?' he sez. 'I'll jes' throw you out.' An' he comes at me, a whoppin' grizzly mind ye, all business-like.

"I whipped out my knife. I always kept a good huntin' knife in them days. It was sharp an' th' very best steel. But I couldn't face thet bear with it to save my soul. I turned an' run out of thar.

"But jes' as soon as I got out in th' sunlight, th' elk made fer me again. By thet time I had begun to realize how danged unpopular I was in them parts. I throwed one look over my shoulder at th' hole. Thar stood thet danged bear right in th' entrance. He was a-guardin' his home, an' he looked worse 'n th' elk.

"Gentlemen, I faced thet elk with nothin' but my knife in my hand. Th' old timers used to say grab th' bull by th' horns, an' thet's jes' whut I done. I jumped right in between them tremendous prongs, an' thar I hung, holdin' on with one hand an' a-slashin' at him in th' neck with t'other.

"It was all I could do to hold on, fer he was a-rarin' an' a-kickin' an' a-buckin' tryin' to throw me off. I had hob-nail shoes on, an' every chance I got I kicked hell outa him.

"Finely, he backs me up against a rock, an' lucky fer me it was flat on top. I lets my feet down, drops my knife an' grabs holt of them horns with both hands. Then it was my stren'th against his'n. An' them days I was strong as an ox.

"Th' elk was weak from bleedin', but he was still as strong as last night's coffee.

"I twisted an' twisted. An' gentlemen, I'm hyar to tell you I twisted thet elk clean to th' grond."

The old man paused and lighted his dead pipe with a splinter from the stove.

79

"What happened then?" I asked amusedly.

Old Sank puffed a few times. "He died with my hands still on his horns. I reck'n I broke his neck. An', gentlemen, them was horns! No wonder he couldn't get in th' bear's den. Sixteen feet from tip to tip. Yes-s-s. . . them was th' days."

I looked at Smitty. He was staring at the old trapper, with that half-cynical smile of his.

"Sank," I said, tolerantly smiling, "those horns are getting bigger and bigger. The last time I heard you tell that tale they were only fifteen feet across."

Old Sank indignantly rose from his chair. "No, sir," he said, emphatically. "You didn't understand me. They was sixteen feet from tip to tip. If you don't believe it, they're in my loft right now."

"Well, I don't believe it," said Smith. "It's impossible."

The old trapper hopped from one foot to the other in his anger. "You don't believe it?" he cried. "Whut you think I am, a liar? Why you little pinhead. I learned to tell th' truth before you was borned!"

"No. I'm not calling you a liar, Sank," said Smith. "But I'll bet just the same those horns weren't sixteen feet."

"Whut'll you bet?" shouted the old man, now thoroughly aroused. "Whut'll you bet?"

Smitty took a roll from his pocket. "Payday yesterday," he remarked, and counted out bills. "There. There's fifty dollars that says those horns of yours in the loft aren't sixteen feet."

"I'll cover it. I'll show you who's a liar!"

Old Sank unlocked a battered old chest in the corner and taking out a handful of greasy bills, gave them to me, to be stakeholder.

"Thar's forty-one dollars," he said. "I'll throw in two fox skins to make fifty. Them skins is worth more'n nine dollars."

Smitty looked at him in surprise. Perhaps the old fellow really was telling the truth. But this was no time to back out.

"All right," he said and gave me his fifty. "Now let's see those horns."

Old Sank took the lantern and led our way up the rickety ladder. The pale light filled the musty loft. "I ain't been up here for a year or two," he said, as he held up the lantern to look around.

"Where are your horns?" Smitty demanded.

The old man looked about him in a dazed way. At the other end of the loft there was a pile of shingles and miscellaneous junk.

"I'm danged!" he said at last, letting the lantern down. "They

80

ain't here."

"What's in that pile of rubbish?" I asked. I walked over and moved boxes aside.

"Here you are, Sank," I said, lifting a pair of horns.

"Are those your horns?" asked Smitty.

The old man looked at them with bewildered eyes.

"Them's deer horns," he said, shaking his head, as though puzzled. "Jes' a four-point buck . . ." He seemed to be searching his memory. Sinking down on a barrel, he scratched his tousled gray hair.

At length he rose and faced his visitors.

"Are those your horns?" Smitty repeated.

"Yep. They're mine. I remember now, boys. It's been over twenty years since I killed that buck. An' th' same day I run into a bear in a cave. An' I killed him. Yes-s-s, I musta killed thet elk some other time. Anyhow, you win th' bet."

"No, I sure don't win your money. Maybe the elk you killed did have sixteen foot horns. Anyway, I can't prove they weren't sixteen feet or eighteen feet. Besides, I wouldn't take your money even if I'd won it."

"The artist," I said, "is worthy of his hire!"

"Whut you mean, artist? I ain't drawed no picture."

"Oh, yes you have," I said. "With words. You're a literary artist, and just don't realize it."

Well, Old Sank was inaccurate in his memory about the horns and the good old days, but was telling the truth about knowing where the animals, including deer, were. With a lot of deer signs around, Smitty and I separated and hunted two ways.

Smitty was not an excellent shot, but he could shoot fairly well, and this seemed to be his day. As in fishing, luck is an important element in hunting. Occasionally, on a poor hunting-luck day, I have thought that the ancient humorous statement about fisherman's luck could be slightly altered and applied to hunting: hunter's luck! A ragged ass and a hungry gut!

I had been hunting without sight of a deer about half an hour when I heard the boom of a heavy-gauge shotgun. I hurried in Smitty's direction to see how lucky he was. Near a large saguaro cactus a big buck lay shot in the chest. With that heavy gun, Smitty had shot well that day.

I resumed my hunting, and had walked another two hours or so when it seemed I *did* have a lucky chance. In the far distance a large animal was climbing a high hill, near its summit. I looked through my binoculars and saw that he was a magnificent buck. Eight points! I knew that he was almost, if not entirely, out of rifle range; but in view of my poor luck that day, I quickly aimed and fired. Then, before I could shoot a second time, he went over the crest. Now I hoped I had not wounded him as I hurried to the top of the hill ahead. There I saw no sign of the deer. And I was relieved to see no red trail of a wound. For a while I hunted around the spot without sight of any deer.

Well, let him go, I thought. A magnificent animal. Who am I to take his life in its prime? I don't need his meat. He does.

I rejoined Old Sank and Smitty. And we muscled his kill to the back of his car, and tied it there. There would be a lot of venison in that big animal's body and part of it would be mine. So the trip was not entirely unsuccessful for me after all.

CHAPTER 9
Always In the Heart

My brother Chester (called "Chet") wrote me one of his rare letters. Several years before he had gone deep into Sonora and there acquired a silver mine, part of which he got by gambling. He was an inveterate part-time gambler, liking to play poker, and skilled and lucky in it. He wrote that he had become a friend of a rebellious general who, with a few other high-ranking generals, was planning another Mexican revolution. The general had advised him to draw his money in gold out of the *Banco de Sonora*, and take it to the United States. Chet wanted to know if I would come and take his gold *pesos* to an Arizona bank. He said he needed to stay there and protect his mine during the coming hostilities, which apparently were about to occur.

We always have been a closely-knit family so I arranged to take some of my "annual leave" and with the help of the Nogales Immigration Inspector in charge, I managed to get papers for my visit in Sonora which permitted me to carry my gun. I went down by the *Sud Pacífico de México* train and Chet met me at the Guaymas station in his old Ford touring car.

In returning, I took what was to be the last train out of that area, carrying Chet's gold in a leather bag. As he had predicted, the war already had come. I was sad to leave my brother in the midst of hostilities, but I knew that he had a good chance of repelling any looters' attacks, for his mine entrance was narrow, cave-like, and he had a one-man arsenal.

I sat in a rather crowded coach of this last train northward for the war's duration, hurrying through the northwestern desert of Mexico. I watched that desert scene speeding past my window, the needle-armed saguaro, and the barbed-spine chollas. All armed to repel attackers. And here was I, armed like the cacti with my pistol at my side, its holster resting on the seat, for the moment taking its weight off my waist. The leather bag of gold was on the floor at my feet.

The rhythmic click-click of wheels over rail joints was about to lull me to sleep when suddenly I was violently thrown into alertness by a fusillade of shots outside. Brakes screeched and the coach hurtled to a standstill. Through the window I saw rifle-carrying Mexican troops in wide, straw sombreros and nondescript uniforms, mostly faded and cactus-torn denim.

"Rebels!" cried the Mexican merchant with the double chin who sat by me. He drew a rubber band-bound sheaf of United States bills from his inside breast pocket, fingered them nervously and uncertainly, then laid them on the floor behind his feet. The rebel troops, led by a young but big-bellied officer, boarded the car. This spur-and-sword-wearing leader was flamboyantly uniformed. He wore epaulets that I thought must represent a rebel general. A cocky young rebel major was by his side. And the three *soldados* who accompanied them had their rifles pointed toward the passengers.

"Friends," the rebel leader said in Spanish, "the Revolution needs funds. Therefore, we are forced to hold up your train, and borrow the money you have, for the cause."

"Therefore!" sneered a young caballero back of me. I had been conscious of this fellow passenger, dressed in picturesque costume, reminiscent of old-time Mexico. He too had a forty-five-calibre pistol, a double-action Colt revolver with a wooden stock probably with a filed hair trigger, I thought, for it was low-slung in a worn, open-top holster at his right. I had noted the numerous notches cut into the wood of the stock, and had heard him boast in Spanish to the lady who was his seat companion about his last gunfight, in self defense, he said.

The general snatched his revolver from its gold-trimmed holster and pointed it down the aisle. "Who sneered?" he demanded, murder in his voice.

Silence like death ensued.

"Who insinuated," the rebel officer continued in angry Spanish, "that General Pereyra does not use this money for the cause?" He waved his pearl-handled revolver, like a cobra ready for attack. "Who dares sneer at the general?"

Still no answer.

The big-bellied officer's helpless anger amused me and I smiled.

"It was you!" shouted the general, turning his revolver toward me. I saw the malevolent danger in that angry face. And suddenly I dropped behind the seat ahead of me. Simultaneously, he fired.

The woman in front of me screamed. Her cry ended in a gurgle as she thumped to the floor.

I drew my automatic, sprang into the aisle, and opened fire. My first shot hit the general, and my second laid him low.

In the coach all was confusion.

"Bravo!" yelled the handsome young caballero. "Good shooting, my friend."

I ducked instinctively as a bullet from the young rebel major's gun cracked by. Smoke was beginning to fill the car. A woman screamed. I rose from behind the seat and calmly aimed at the major who was excitedly pumping bullets in my direction. But before I could pull the trigger, a shot came from behind, and the rebel officer pitched forward without a moan.

"Siempre en el corazón!" the young caballero yelled. And then in English, as if boastfully interpreting for me, the North American, "Always in the heart!"

I whirled. The picturesque young man, smoking revolver in hand, had leaped into the aisle in back of me.

"Bravo, yourself," I said. "Now, let's get the hell out of here!"

So saying, I opened fire on the three soldiers, aiming at their legs. But one quickly fell, killed by a bullet from the caballero's gun. Then the other two beat a hasty retreat from the car.

I hurriedly reloaded my gun, grabbed the handles of the heavy leather bag in my left hand, and ran out, the young Mexican close behind.

We descended into a mass of soldiery. Then, running side by side, we cut our way up the track with bullets. Even while shooting, I noted that every time my companion fired, a soldier fell. Briefly, I wondered who this stranger was, who was so expert with the pistol.

A few yards beyond the engine a gravel-decked bridge spanned a canyon. We turned to the right, plunged into the big ravine, and began running down its boulder-strewn course.

A soldier stationed on the bridge opened fire with a Winchester. I whirled to return his fire. I either missed or wounded the man, and was about to shoot again when a bullet from the soldier's rifle struck my right arm. I dropped my forty-five. Desperately conscious that the fellow would fire again, I dropped the bag, stooped and picked up the revolver in my left hand. Could I shoot before the bullet came?

In the meantime, my companion was quickly reloading his revolver. Now he finished, and hurriedly raised the gun. Without seeming to aim, he pulled the trigger. The soldier fell, his rifle discharging as death deadened his trigger finger.

"Always in the heart!" said the young Mexican again. "Pronto shoots and lives!"

"Many thanks, *compadre*." I picked up my bag with my left hand and I thought, Pronto, eh? Somewhere I've heard that name.

"It's nothing," Pronto was saying. "But you are wounded, my friend, no?" He took a silk handkerchief from his pocket. "I shall bandage it, no?"

"Bandage, *hell*! Man, *let's get out of here!*"

We ran down the canyon, and when out of sight of the bridge slowed to a fast walk.

Just before dusk we came to an adobe hut by the canyon. A Mexican woman came to the door. Her face was prematurely old, and her dark-brown eyes had the meek patience of a long-suffering woman. She wore a coarse black dress that nearly dragged the ground.

A pretty teen-aged, somewhat plump daughter, in a short red dress, smiled at us two strangers while her mother talked.

The old woman did not hesitate about lodging the strangers for the night. She was but a poor widow, she told us, but she never turned anyone away from her door. She looked at my wound, and clucked sympathetically. "María Magdalena," she called.

The daughter ceased flirting with Pronto, whose bold, dark eyes were on her. "Yes, Mama,," she said, coming into the lean-to kitchen.

"The Norteamericano gentleman is hurt. Get water, and wash his wound. Then dress it with a piece of your old petticoat."

María immediately turned her sparkling-brown-eyed attention to me, a norteamericano, and so probably wealthy and was very flirtatious as she complied with her mother's instructions.

"What is your friend's name?" she asked in Spanish, looking up at me as she tied the bandage and gave my arm a tender pat.

I felt a vague resentment against her for speaking of my companion at this time. But I said: "He calls himself *Pronto*. He's probably the best shot in Mexico for whatever that sadly means."

"I knew he was very brave," she said softly. "He would shoot quick for his love for he has the way of a gran señor."

I turned, and walked into the main room of the hut.

My new friend had laid his high-crowned sombrero on one of the pallets in the corner; and, sitting on the packed-clay floor with his back against the adobe wall, he was entertaining the older woman with a tale of our escape from the train. He was dwelling on each little detail, and stretching the truth some with a great deal of flowery eloquence. Nevertheless, I could not help liking the man.

Pronto looked up as I entered. "And here," he said in Spanish, "is one very brave gentleman. He is a very good shot, my friend. Even better than Pronto and Pronto is a very good shot. Well, maybe not better but just as good."

The woman said they were proud to know such brave gentlemen and that their mean little household was safe while such protectors as these lodged beneath their roof. "Might I ask, sir," she said to me, "what are the names of the gentlemen who do me the honor of stopping in my house?"

"My name, Señora, is Ricardo Morton."

"Mohrtone, Señor Mohrtone." She looked inquiringly at my companion. "And you, Señor?"

"Yes," I said. "What is your name, compadre?"

"Qué le hace!" he replied, using a common fatalistic expression of Mexico. "What does it matter?" he shrugged. And then he added another fatalistic Mexican expression, "No importa. But I have been called nicknames. And one of these is Pronto — Quick, with the gun; understand?"

"Pronto — Pronto what?" I asked.

"Just Pronto, my friend. You know, Pronto, Pronto Smith, Pronto Jones, Pronto García. Qué le hace? No importa."

"It seems to me I have heard of a Pronto in the United States."

"How funny, my friend. This is the United States, no?" he laughed. "United States of Mexico, no?"

"You son-of-a-gun, Pronto, don't you ever take any thing in life seriously?"

Pronto shrugged. "No. Why take life serious? It is very funny. A big joke."

"And now, Tía Paulita," he said in Spanish to our hostess. "Please, let us eat. Pronto is hungry. And so is my friend, I am sure."

He rose and looked intently at the girl María Magdalena. "Ah, my Señorita, how very, very beautiful you are!"

She smiled, and half-turned her graceful back to us with a swaying motion of her hips, looking at us over her shoulder. Tía Paulita watched awhile with proud interest before she went to prepare a meal of tortillas and beans. My daughter, she probably thought, will never be an old maid, starving in her old age.

Pronto suddenly turned and striding gracefully to the corner, picked up the old guitar there. Propping one foot on the wood-box, he tuned the instrument and began to play and sing an old Spanish love song. Throbbing with a painful, indefinable something that haunted me with a vague feeling, as of something long ago, nearly lost. Music of Old Spain, of a young man who had lived wildly, with a song on his lips and a pistol in his hand!

Be careful, I thought. Don't glorify him too much, likeable as he is. He probably is a criminal.

María began to dance with a swaying, graceful motion. "I knew it," Pronto said in Spanish. "I always know a good dancer."

Smiling, she picked up his wide-brimmed black hat, laid it on the packed-adobe floor, and danced around it.

At length the musician gently laid down the guitar, his slender fingers caressing the cheap instrument. "Pronto travels too much on horseback. Cannot carry a guitar. Danger. Ride too fast and always in trouble."

Later, in the light of a candle, as I lay on the pallet Tía Paulita had spread on the clay floor, I turned over and stared at my roommate on the nearby pallet. With his jackknife he was cutting notches on the wooden handle of his revolver; one, two, three, the number of men he had killed that day. And again I noted that many notches were there. In the dim light they looked to be about six or seven, in addition to the three new ones. My suspicion about my new friend was being confirmed.

A week oozed by, as time has a way of doing in languorous, summertime Mexico and my wound had healed.

We arranged to buy two burros from Tía Paulita. Nothing was said about the price but she knew she would be well paid.

The next morning Pronto and I prepared to leave. María had tears in her eyes, and Tía Paulita looked sad. It would be lonely with the two young caballeros gone.

I opened the bag of gold. "My brother told me to take expenses of the trip out of this," I remarked to Pronto. And I took a small handful of the gold pieces and laid them on the table for the old woman. And then another, larger amount to pay for the burros. Then I handed a few pesos to María.

Tía Paulita stared at the gold, and shook her head, "But, it is too much. You take some of it back."

"It is all for you, Tía," Pronto said. "Pronto and his friend are good to their friends and bad to their enemies."

Our leavetaking involved as much embracing as if the little family were our lifelong friends.

I mounted my burro. "Come on, Pronto."

We had ridden some distance in silence, when I spoke, "All right, Pronto. Come out of the dumps; and watch where we're going. I think you shouldn't go to the States. But you say you are going. So, it's up to you to help guide us up these canyons to the line. I'm not certain of the way myself."

Pronto continued to ride with downcast face.

"I will come back to that girl," he announced, and I was surprised to recognize a husky note in his voice. "I will come back, for she is nice and beautiful. As beautiful as a rainbow!"

"You won't come back to anything if we run into those revolutionaries. Wake up! A man who killed a major and has a *compadre* who killed a general better watch his step."

Pronto smiled with that elemental magnetism that frequently drew others to him. "You are a good shot, my friend. You and Pronto have a good time, no? I show you how to get gold. Then Pronto go back for María Magdalena."

After a silence, he repeated, "You and Pronto have a good time, no?"

"No, Pronto, I'm sorry for I like you, but I saw the notches in your gun. You kill too much for me."

"But why, why? They kill you if you don't kill them."

"Well, I'll tell you, I think every person has some good in him, and every time I have to kill a man I feel I have killed part of myself."

"Man, you are strange."

"No, not really so strange. I know other men who have had to kill in duty who feel sad about it all. This life is complex, my friend. I don't like to preach to any person. But, Pronto, you should settle down, take care of a family, live in peace."

No reply. Then after riding in silence a while, Pronto began to sing:

Allá en el Rancho grande,
Allá en donde vivía! Ah-yy . . .Ja-Ja-jahy!
Había una rancherita,
Qué alegre me decía, que alegre me decía . . .!

He's eternally juvenile, I thought.

Two weeks later, clothes cactus-torn, we rode in the moonlight to the spot where the trail forks before crossing the International Line into the United States.

I dismounted. "Well, Pronto," I said, making an effort to speak lightly. "Here's where we part. I take this trail to the left and you take the right. It will be safer for you."

Pronto's eyebrows lifted in surprise. "But why, my friend? Pronto does not want to leave you. We will go together. Pronto will show you how to get much gold. We will have a good time together."

"Just has to be, *compadre*. I don't like it at all, but our trails have to separate here. I have come to like you, you son-of-a-gun, like a brother. Just like a brother!" I repeated, and cleared my throat. Then to relieve my emotion, "Damn it! You take that trail to the right, I'm telling you, and I'm taking this one to the left. And you wait behind me, Pronto, till I get almost to the line fence, before you even start. I don't want to see you cross that line into the United States."

"But why?" Pronto repeated.

"It just isn't safe, Pronto, not safe for you if I see you in the States."

We shook hands. "And listen," I continued, "When you go down the hill, be careful not to wake up the guard in the guardhouse there."

With that I strode away, leaving my burro free to roam at will.

Some fifty yards down the hill I heard a sound behind me. I whirled, and was surprised to see Pronto following on foot.

I waited until the other had caught up with me, and then I said, "*Compadre*, I need to tell you something."

Pronto was silent.

"I know who you are. I have known all along, I guess; but I wouldn't admit it even to myself, because I liked you. You're Pronto Bernal, the bandit that's been raising hell in these parts for the last three years. Both sides of the line. Always robbing alone and infernally quick with the gun. No wonder there are so many notches on your gun. There's a bounty on your head for four thousand dollars, and the man who arrests you alive would get five thousand."

Pronto laughed. "Worth a little more alive than dead! But, no man will ever arrest Pronto alive."

"No, but they'll sure as hell get you dead, Pronto. Why in the world don't you quit this foolishness and settle down to work?"

"I starved once, working like a slave. I will not starve again."

"Well, then, why don't you quit?

"Nobody can shoot like Pronto. Except maybe you. I want you to be my partner. We can rob a bank tomorrow, we can rob trains, banks, and get much gold. And then, back to Mexico!"

"What an irony of fate! Asking me to be a robber! If old McGuire could hear this, he'd never quit talking!"

Pronto's brow became sullen. "Who is McGuire?"

"Don't take offense at what I say, ever. I should have said who he is. Of course, you don't know. He's a deputy sheriff, a fairly good officer, but he talks too much. And he's in the shadow of a really mean one, Undersheriff Pellet. Don't ever get near him, Pronto. He wouldn't try to arrest you alive. He'd try to kill you any way he could."

"It's not possible, I would kill him first!"

"And get yourself in awful trouble. I'd have to be on the posse that went after you. You haven't known who I am, Pronto. I'm a sworn officer of the United States Border Patrol." Then I added with a smile, "That's the United States of the North."

Pronto seemed stunned as I continued. "I would hate to have to go after you. My good friend, who saved my life twice but my sworn duty comes ahead of everything. Including you or if necessary my own life."

"But you're going through a hole in the fence, just like any other smuggler."

"Yes, I'm sorry to say. I didn't bring my badge. And the gold is not mine to risk. I think there's no duty on it. But anyway, I'll declare it at the Customhouse tomorrow. Now let's vamoose. You wait here until I'm gone, understand?"

I had gone perhaps another twenty yards, when I turned. In the moonlight I saw that Pronto was following not far behind. "Damn it, Pronto! You take that other trail!"

If the other answered, I did not know it. For another, more important matter came to hand. A figure in the moonlight that had looked like a saguaro cactus suddenly moved. It was a man. He raised a rifle to his shoulder and yelled in Spanish, "Halt or I shoot!"

For a fleeting instant, I thought of yelling that I was a U.S. Border Patrol officer. But then I thought of the gold, my ragged condition, and the reputation of Mexican jails. So, on the spur of the moment I dashed for the hole in the fence. As I fell to crawl through, the rifle cracked. But I was not hit.

Pronto, who had been advancing warily toward the guard, must have drawn his revolver. I was crawling on through the fence. Hastily I glanced backward. The guard was on one knee, taking no chances of missing.

True to his name, Pronto was quicker. His forty-five roared and the guard fell, doubtless shot through the heart.

On the other side of the fence I turned and saw the guard was dead. I shook my head sadly, and muttered, "Saved again by the killing gun of Pronto Bernal!"

It was not long after I was back on duty that word came that Pronto Bernal was back in the country and had robbed a bank, stolen ten thousand dollars and a horse. Pellet and McGuire got the news first and without bothering to inform the Border Patrol. Obviously, they hoped to capture Pronto and collect the reward and not have to share it. Unfortunately for them, they did catch up and were outmaneuvered and gunned down.

A posse was quickly assembled and I was included. We followed Pronto's tracks across the canyon where he had shot and killed Pellet and McGuire, across a mesa and toward a peculiarly shaped hill with steep sides. Halfway up there was a small cave with a small open, flat place in front. He had left his horse at the foot of the hill and started climbing the hill when I spotted him through my binoculars.

"He went into the cave up Sombrero Hill, boys," I announced.

"You know now, Richard," drawled Joe Platt, removing his wide Border Patrol hat and replacing it at a more picturesque angle, "it ain't gonna be easy to get Pronto Bernal out of that cave."

"I know how we can get him," said Deputy Arnold Briggs, a little man with a somewhat shifty eye.

"How's that?" I asked.

"Don't let him know we suspect where he is. Just ride on by, and then slip back by the other side of the hill, and when he shows himself, let him have it with the Winchester."

I glared at him; and Briggs shifted his glance.

"We're here to arrest this man," I reproved, "not to murder him."

The little man's face became sullen, and I could see that his frequently hot temper was boiling within him.

I had not forgotten former encounters with this ruthless officer. There was a long story back of his hatred of me. It began when I arrested his brother, Max, for smuggling, coming through a hole in the fence, and was conducting him, not handcuffed, to the U.S. Customs

Office for their filing of charges. Then we were met by Deputy Sheriff Briggs; and relying on help from a brother officer, he pleaded with me to free his first-offense brother. But to no avail. Then, seeing his chance, Max tried to escape to a nearby hole in the border fence. But I quickly fired, hit him in the leg, and he doubled up in pain. Then with a pistol at his back, I conducted him on to the Customs Office. Ever since that time, Deputy Sheriff Briggs apparently had hated me. I knew he, with his fierce temper, was one I needed to watch for possible foul play.

We three officers dismounted at what we thought was a safe distance from the bottom of the hill and studied the precipice, and the steep, narrow ravine. Border Patrolman Joe Platt, from Texas, advanced toward it. Then suddenly a shot rang out, and the bullet kicked up dust back of him. He quickly withdrew.

"Too far for him to hit with a pistol, I reckon," Joe drawled.

"He was just warning us," I said grimly. "If he'd tried, one of us would be dead now. He's a better shot than any man here. Deadly! I know that hombre."

"You don't say, Richard," Joe said. "When did you tangle with Pronto Bernal?"

"I haven't yet. Well, how are we going to get him out of there alive? That's the question."

We withdrew to a safer spot in a little gully.

Then as we watched, I saw Pronto's head cautiously appear near the upraised ridge at the rim of the cleft. Arnold Briggs quickly raised his rifle and fired. The head retreated.

"Quit shooting, Briggs!" I snapped. "If we can't arrest him alive or kill him in a fair fight, we just won't take him. We're not murderers."

"You're *some* officer, ain't you!" jeered Briggs.

"I'm warning you now, Briggs. If you shoot that man in the back, I'm taking you in for murder."

"Come on, fellows," Joe urged. "Let's not fight among ourselves. Not now!"

We held a conference and considered several plans to reach Bernal's stronghold, only to discard each. At last, I said it would be best to starve Pronto out. And I was about to ask Joe to go back to Nogales and bring the other two Border Patrol Inspectors stationed there to help as night guards, when a rock fell ahead of us and rolled into the gully. A scrap of paper was tied to it with a piece of string. I grabbed it and translated aloud the Spanish note: "If it is so that you want to arrest me and not die on the way up, one of your *quicos* come up at a time. If only one man comes, Pronto gives his word to Morton that he will not shoot him on the way up. Ricardo better not come first. He better wait. Pronto Bernal."

"Well, now what do you know about that!" Joe said. "Regular Chinese puzzle, ain't he." Then, "I reckon, Mr. Briggs, it's up to you and me to flip a coin to see who goes."

"I'm not flippin' no coin," said Briggs, nervously. "Let Morton go, if he's so all-fired bound to die as a hero."

I did not answer, but checked the looseness of my automatic .45 in its worn holster.

"Not so fast, Richard," Joe Platt said easily. "That note says you better wait, and that fellow up yonder means what he says. He'd shoot you if you went. I ain't gonna let you go. I'm gonna go myself."

Before I could make a move, Platt was out of the gully and hastening toward the hill. I started to follow, but thought better of it, and crouched back to wait.

Briggs and I sat tensely as we watched Joe's course up the precipice. At length, the climber came to a point opposite the cave. Here he left the ravine and laboriously climbed the upraised ridge in front of the cave, the roof of which could just be seen from below. Then he disappeared from view. We two sat there, tense, listening.

Suddenly two revolver shots were heard, close together. Then silence. Followed by Briggs, I sprang out of the gully and ran ahead to a small mound. From this spot we could better see beyond the cave rim. Nothing but little rocks and boulders could be made out on its surface. The silence of the hard, manless, cactus-thorned desert hung over the sombrero-shaped hill. The brief mid-summer rains and the amazing, prodigal beauty of the desert flowers had come and gone. Up above, a buzzard circled in the brazen late-summer bowl of the sky. It was mid-afternoon, and the heat was stifling.

For several minutes we stood there. Then, without a word to Briggs, I went to the ravine, and began climbing up from ledge to ledge. I looked backwards once; Arnold Briggs had hastened to his horse, taken his thirty-thirty rifle from his saddle, and now was following me in the climb. I didn't like having my back turned to him. That reward money doubtless was tempting to him.

Tensely, I checked every object at the cave entrance the instant I came to it. To my left, by a lone saguaro cactus, lay my friend Joe

Platt, dead. Almost simultaneously, I saw my erstwhile friend rise from where he had been sitting at the mouth of the cave, smoking a cigarette. I looked at Pronto's small right hand that hung near the low-slung holster.

"Well, *amigo mío*," Pronto said with his magnetic smile. "Or is it that you don't come as a friend to Pronto now you are in the North?"

"Pronto, you don't understand," I said, shaking my head. "I am an officer of the law. I've got to arrest you. Don't you see?"

"No. No, I don't see. An officer of law, you change it a little, no? You let me go, my friend," he argued, earnestly, "and I never will rob any more in your country."

"Let you go, Pronto? After you killed three men in this country?"

"Nobody will ever know anything about it."

"They won't, huh? What about that man I left down there?"

"You tell him you let me go. That's all."

"No. You come with me, Pronto. You're under arrest."

Suddenly without any warning, Pronto's face set in a hard line and he snatched his gun.

My right hand moved fast, and I fired from my hip. Pronto swayed, gasped and struggled to stand upright. He had turned and was facing the mesa. He pointed his revolver below with a leaden hand and fired once.

Almost simultaneouly there came an explosion from the nearby ridge. A bullet pinged through the crown of my hat. I whirled and looked below. Arnold Briggs was falling from the ridge.

"He tried to kill you, my friend," said the swaying figure with the smoking revolver still in hand. "But Pronto killed him. *Siempre en el corazón!*"

The revolver dropped, and he sank to a sitting position. Then he spoke in Spanish, "Please do me the favor, *amigo mío,* of sending the Mexican gold in my pocket to María. Her address is there in my pocket." He switched to English, "Pronto no need rob bank no more. No need cut off cactus thorns. And Pronto starve no more."

He fell on his side. In grief, I knelt by him. "I'm sorry, Pronto," I said, tears in my eyes. "So very, very sorry. I shot too soon!"

Up above, the buzzard still wheeled in the hard blue bowl of the sky, waiting, hoping to conquer bodies by the cactus thorns. The heat of the semi-desert, of the harsh and forbidding land that lay all around, was stifling. Before me lay the body of my carefree friend who had lived: *Always in the heart!*

www.ingramcontent.com/pod-product-compliance
Lightning Source LLC
Chambersburg PA
CBHW031145090426
42738CB00008B/1224